GUIDE TO
TOY
COLLECTING

GUIDE TO
TOY
COLLECTING

BY HARRY L. RINKER

Collins
An Imprint of HarperCollinsPublishers

DEDICATED TO

Those who believe in the principle that he who dies with the biggest pile of toys wins,
Those who saved their childhood toys,
Those who bought back their childhood toys plus all the toys they should have received in the first place,
And, most importantly,
Those who still get down on the floor and play with their toys, sharing the experience with their grandchildren and future generations, fully understanding that in doing so they themselves never really have to admit to growing up.

HarperCollins books may be purchased for educational, business, or sales promotional use. For information please write: Special Markets Department, HarperCollins Publishers, 10 East 53rd Street, New York, NY 10022.

FIRST EDITION

The name of the "Smithsonian," "Smithsonian Institution," and the sunburst logo are registered trademarks of the Smithsonian Institution.

Produced by BAND-F Ltd, www.band-f.com
President / Partner: f-stop fitzgerald
Director of Development: Karen Jones
Production Editor: Mie Kingsley
Production Manager and Interior Design: Maria Fernandez
Digital Art Technician: Weston Minissali

Library of Congress Cataloging-in-Publication Data

Rinker, Harry L.
  Guide to toy collecting / by Harry L. Rinker. — 1st ed.
    p. cm.
  Includes bibliographical references.
  ISBN 978-0-06-134141-0
  1. Toys--Collectors and collecting. I. Title.

  NK9509.R56 2008
  688.7'2075--dc22

2007027769

08 09 10 11 12   TOP   10 9 8 7 6 5 4 3 2 1

CONTENTS

INTRODUCTION

Toys and childhood memories are inexorably linked. Toys figure in our most positive early memories. The memories often begin with the sense of discovery and acquisition and center around the play and care involved. While many childhood toys are lost, their memories are never erased. They remain with us throughout our life. One must only think of Orson Welles's "Rosebud" to be reminded of the powerful feelings and emotional pull that toys can inspire.

Given this, it should come as no surprise that when the collecting bug strikes, many collectors decide to buy back their childhood toys. Eventually, collecting interests may broaden to include movie, music, and television memorabilia and more. No matter where collecting interests reside, the collecting principles and techniques learned from collecting toys will influence collecting habits for life.

Toys Are Not Only for Children

Most believe that adults do not play with toys. Toys are for children. In reality, toys are for everyone. Toys are designed for play. If you start playing with toys you'll find that life appears very different when you are down on the floor. Do not be surprised to discover you are having fun.

Once you have rediscovered how much fun it is to play with toys, you may start yearning for your childhood toys. It is now time to raid the attic and basement at your home. If you are

Gene Autry, Hopalong Cassidy, the Lone Ranger, and Roy Rogers were among the most popular "B" movie western and television cowboy heroes of the early 1950s. William Boyd, a.k.a., Hopalong Cassidy, licensed over 2,500 products.

lucky, some of your childhood toys survived. Hopefully, your favorite toys are among them. If not, it is time to hunt for them.

Buying back your childhood toys can be expensive. It most certainly will be if you whip out your wallet and start buying every toy you see. The good news is that buying back your childhood does not have to be expensive. If you have patience—few collectors do—and are technologically savvy, you can reacquire most of your childhood toys at reasonable prices.

There are no fixed prices in the antiques and collectibles marketplace. Do not be surprised when you find the same toy priced differently at an antiques mall, flea market, garage sale, or toy show. Comparison

shopping pays when buying toys. Resist the urge to buy the first example you see unless you know it is well priced.

Understanding the intricacies of the toy market separates the novice toy collector from the toy connoisseur.

What Is a Toy?

Defining what constitutes a toy can be a difficult undertaking. *Webster's Ninth New Collegiate Dictionary* defines a toy as "something for a child to play with." This definition is too narrow. Toys designed for family play involve parents as well as children. Toys are not child-specific.

Webster's New World Dictionary of the American Language, Second College Edition defines a toy as "Any article to play with, esp. a plaything for children." This definition is too broad. When a young child gets into a kitchen cabinet and starts playing with the pots and pans or converts a discarded large cardboard

Mrs. Beasley, Buffy's doll from the television show *Family Affair*, was popular with young girls in the late 1960s. Family Affair, starring Brian Keith as Bill Davis, Anissa Jones as Buffy, and Sabastian Cabot as Mr. Jiles French, aired on CBS from September 12, 1966 to September 9, 1971.

Technically speaking, a doll is a toy. However, dolls, such as this 24-inch-high Philadelphia baby by Sheppard Company, are far more likely to be found at a doll show than a toy show.

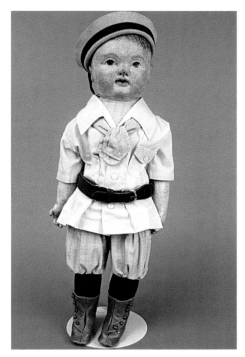

box into a makeshift fort, he or she is obviously involved in play. Yet, no one would define these objects as toys.

For the purpose of this book, a toy is any object specifically designed, manufactured, and used for play. This is a broad definition and includes dolls, games, and puzzles. This broad definition runs counter to developments within the toy-collecting community, in which items are being classified into increasingly specific categories.

Doll collecting has become a world unto itself. Doll collectors have their own separate collectors' clubs, literature, and show circuit. Dolls are no longer found and sold at toy shows. Games and puzzles also are in the process of separating themselves from the tra-

ditional world of toy collecting. Game and puzzle collectors have formed their own collectors' clubs. While games and puzzles are still sold at traditional toy shows, game and puzzle collectors find the hunting is often better at advertising or paper shows.

Ultimately, an object is a toy if you play with it for fun and entertainment. You instinctively know a toy when you see one. Curiosity demands that you pick up the toy and play with it. It challenges your imagination and your play skills.

The late 1940s through the 1960s was View-Master's Golden Age. The Model C viewer became a classic toy. View-Master obtained licenses for popular cartoons and television programs and the projector allowed children to mimic their parent's 35mm slide shows.

Origin of a Classic Toy

In 1903, Morris and Rose Mitchom founded the Ideal Toy & Novelty Company to meet the demand for a new toy. The Mitchoms, Russian immigrants, owned a store in Brooklyn, New York. Inspired by the story of President Theodore Roosevelt's refusal to shoot a bear cub on a Mississippi hunt, Rose hand-crafted a soft, jointed bear and displayed it in the store window. Sales were brisk. Morris wrote President Roosevelt asking if he could name the bear, "Teddy's Bear." The President agreed, while acknowledging that he felt his name would add little to the toy's value. The "s" was dropped. The Teddy Bear became part of toy history.

Vehicle collectors eagerly seek German, lithography tin vehicles, such as this circa 1900 open touring car. Because of their low survival rate, collectors consider any example in fine or better condition as a classic toy.

Why Collect Toys?

There is absolutely no requirement that you have to have a reason for collecting toys. If you want to do it, then do it.

To rephrase the question: "What motivates a person to collect toys?"

Nostalgia is the biggest factor; generations of toy collectors collect the toys associated with their childhoods. While today's youngsters are accustomed to receiving "new" toys, older collectors, who grew up in the age of hand-me-down toys, appreciated the toys of their parents' and grandparents' generation. And they played with those toys more. Many twenty-first-century youngsters are used to owning an abundance of toys, and in this day and age there are a huge variety of toys from which to choose. As a result, the amount of play time spent with a specific toy has decreased. In a collecting category where nostalgia and memory are crucial, this will most certainly impact what and how toys are collected in the future.

There is a danger in becoming a collector, especially a toy collector. Once you are hooked, it can be almost impossible to stop. Initially many new toy collectors focus on reacquiring the toys they once owned. However, as the collection grows, it may expand to all the toys the collector once coveted. A collection may not be

Youngsters growing up in the twenty-first century play with Super Soakers and others types of water guns. After a summer of play, water guns such as this Teenage Mutant Ninja Turtles Don's Sewer Squirter are likely to end up abandoned in the garage or toy box.

considered complete until it contains every toy the collector ever wanted and more.

There are toy collectors who fall in love with a specific toy group—such as pressed steel vehicles or toys made during World War II—or toy manufacturer—such as Matchbox or Mattel. These collectors build type collections. Their goal is simple—acquire one of every example made. In many cases, the time periods represented by the toys in their collection far exceed their own toy memories. Due to the diligence and thoroughness of these collectors, some of the best toy study collections are found in private hands and not museums or other public institutions.

Investment potential continues to grow as a prime motivator to collect toys. Just like the T-206 Honus Wagner baseball cards, many

An Idea That Was Fifty Years Ahead of Its Time

John Wright, son of the famous architect Frank Lloyd Wright, traveled with his father to Tokyo, where his father was involved in designing the famed Imperial Hotel. John, inspired by the overlapping construction techniques used in the building's foundation, created Lincoln Logs in 1916. He patented the toy on August 31, 1920. Hasbro's Playskool division still manufactures Lincoln Logs.

In the late 1860s Joel Ellis of Vermont made wooden toys under the brand names of Cooperative Manufacturing Company; Ellis, Britton and Eaton; and Vermont Novelty Works. One of these toys was a collection of small wooden logs that could be assembled to construct several different buildings. Alas for Ellis, the children of that era did not find his construction toy appealing, and it disappeared from the toy scene.

Popular toys, such as Lincoln Logs, continue to survive. Lincoln Logs will celebrate its ninetieth birthday in 2010, not the oldest toy in continuous production by any means.

high-end toys are now collected as investment commodities rather than objects with which to play. Major auction houses and toy auctioneers tout toys as a "safe investment." Other sources, such as television appraisal shows, indirectly support this concept.

The number of individuals who have the funds to participate in the upper end of the toy market is limited. The general public participates by hoarding new toys and participating in the speculative secondary markets that result, although the Beanie Baby debacle appears to have temporarily curbed the hoarder/speculators.

What Does Toy Collecting Have to Offer?

Toy collecting allows you to express and even create your own unique personality. This is one of the wonderful things about toy collecting. No two collections, even if focused on the same toy, are ever identical. What toys you choose to collect, which you decide to display, and how you talk about them is an expression of who you are. Collecting, managing, and playing with your toys can be a peaceful refuge from life's stressors.

Toy collecting allows you to experience the thrill of the hunt. In the past, the hunt was limited to trips to antiques malls, flea markets, garage sales, toy shows, and shops. Today, the hunting ground is far more likely to be accessed by your computer. It really makes no difference where you hunt, so long as it brings you pleasure.

Toy collecting is not an American phenomenon. Many of America's earliest toys came from Europe. Today American designed and licensed toys are sold worldwide, a trend that began immediately following World War II. American collectors often compete on the Internet with collectors from around the globe for the same toy.

Toy collecting will broaden your geographic knowledge, not only of the United States, but of the world. Vacations can be planned around major toy shows or visits to the communities where favorite toys were made. Toy collecting is a great way to become part of the global community.

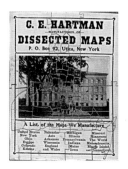

Dissected maps represent some of the earliest American-made jigsaw puzzles. Because they had an educational focus, children were allowed to play with them on Sundays. Eventually, they worked their way into the classroom where they were used to teach geography.

Through their collections, all toy collectors become curators, committed to preserving and understanding the past. Historical societies, historic sites, and museums have limited resources. They cannot collect everything. Private collectors are the leaders in preserving a country's common culture and everyday objects.

There is a great deal of camaraderie in the toy collecting community. Whether at a collectors' club convention or toy shop, toy collectors tend to congregate. This is not to suggest there is a distinct toy collector personality. Far from it! If anything, individuality prevails.

Most toy collectors do not look upon their collections as their retirement plan, as most do not plan to sell them. Yet, as a toy collection grows, it becomes a tangible asset, either to the collector or his or her heirs.

Finally, toy collecting serves as a link between generations. When you attend a toy

Ten Reasons to Collect Toys

1.   Enhance your sense of individuality
2.   Escape from the pressures of everyday life
3.   Experience the thrill of the hunt
4.   Increase geographic knowledge
5.   Become part of the global community
6.   Preserve and understand the past
7.   Achieve personal recognition
8.   Share camaraderie
9.   Make a tangible investment
10. Build a link between generations

train show, you cannot help noticing the number of grandparent-grandchild pairings. The concept of play inherent in toys is an unspoken language that bridges any generation gap.

What This Book Has to Offer

This book is an introduction to the joys of toy collecting. Its goal is to point you in the right direction, provide tips and insider advice, and show you the wide range of collecting possibilities, from historical toys to current ones. It explores where to find toys and how to determine what they are worth, as well as how to display toys and keep records so that your toys may be enjoyed for generations to come.

Toy collectors often spend many hours researching the history of the toys in their collection. They love sharing this information with other collectors.

CHAPTER ONE

THE HISTORY OF TOYS

Toys play a myriad of roles, especially as learning tools to foster creativity, critical thinking, and imagination through play. Some toys assist children in acquiring the skills necessary to socialize and understand fairness. Others can help improve physical skills and provide a positive outlet for a child's energy.

Examining a culture's toys allows anthropologists, sociologists, and other researchers to theorize about a people's values and beliefs. Toys can also offer a historical perspective, such as when dolls are clothed in period costumes and boats and wheeled vehicles mimic their larger contemporaries.

Ancient Toys

In antiquity, many toys were actually objects used to play games, such as balls. Boys' games tended to be team-focused and more highly competitive than games played by girls. Marbles is one of the earliest known games. A game similar to chess was played by the Babylonians as early as 4000 B.C.

The issue of whether an object is or is not a toy continues to perplex anthropologists. Is a small toy horse figurine a toy or a cult object?

OPPOSITE: Toys are meant for play. Buildings, people, and other accessories make a toy train platform come alive. How they are displayed makes each platform unique.

This Guntherman, German, clock-work automobile has a litho-graphed tin body style that was popular at the beginning of the twentieth century.

games included Senet, closely related to backgammon, and House and Jackal, similar to the modern board game of Goose.

Greece and Rome

The toy vocabulary expanded during the Greek and Roman eras. Infants had rattles in the shapes of animals. Boys played with wooden swords and rode hobby horses. Dolls, often jointed, were made of cloth or wax. Unisex toys like rolling wooden hoops and stilts became popular.

The Greeks and Romans continued to play Senet. Greek and Roman children played a dice-like game in which four pieces were thrown, resulting in 35 different scoring possibilities. The dice were made from the knucklebones of a sheep or goat and the game ultimately evolved into modern-day jacks.

Asia

Kites were popular in China by 1000 B.C. In A.D. 969 early playing cards were found, made of clay and tin. Later examples were made of wood. The Chinese and Japanese are credited with the creation of the whipped top.

Egypt

Small toy boats carved from wood were found in a child's tomb in pre-Dynastic Egypt. By the time of the Dynasties, toys made of bone, ceramics (especially clay), ivory, stone, and wood were common. Balls were made of glazed papyrus or painted wood. Girls played with Nubian dolls. Some dolls even had jointed limbs. Toy animals were lifelike in appearance. Some were animated, such as a crocodile with a moving jaw or a man washing or kneading dough. A dancing dwarf toy, manipulated by strings and pulleys, was found in a Middle Kingdom, twelfth Dynasty tomb. Tipcat, a game in which a stick with tapered ends is struck to drive it into the air so the player can attempt to hit it, dates to the Middle Kingdom.

Board games also were popular. Mehen, the game of snake, was played on a surface depicting a snake whose body was divided into squares. Playing pieces resembled lions and lionesses. Other

The Oldest Toy

What is the oldest toy? While historians disagree, the yo-yo is the toy most often cited. Archaeologists have found yo-yos in sites in ancient Greece. The Chinese claim they had a version of the toy that dates even earlier.

By the 1700s the yo-yo, known as the jou-jou, was a favorite at the French court. The idea spread to England. Victorian children loved the yo-yo. By the end of the nineteenth century, several American inventors filed yo-yo patents.

The 1930s was the yo-yo's golden age in America, thanks in large part to the efforts of Donald Duncan and Pedro Flores. Duncan, a master marketer, saw Flores demonstrating the yo-yo in Los Angeles and bought Flores's struggling Yo-Yo Manufacturing Company. Duncan hired a group of "yo-yo men" to travel the country demonstrating basic yo-yo tricks such as "walking the dog."

Presidents John F. Kennedy, Lyndon Johnson, and Richard Nixon all enjoyed playing with the yo-yo.

Medieval and Renaissance Toys

Until the later half of the twentieth century, many scholars thought that children growing up in the Middle Ages (A.D. 476 - A.D. 1450) experienced very little childhood. A series of recent discoveries found buried in the Thames River near London has revealed that as early as A.D. 1200 children enjoyed metal toys in the shapes of cannons and guns, figures, and miniature furniture such as cauldrons, frying plans, jugs, and stools. Middle Age metal toys were made from pewter, an alloy of lead

English and German mass-produced toys dominated the marketplace by the mid-nineteenth century. Availability and affordability resulted in toys becoming popular birthday and holiday gifts.

and tin, which deteriorates easily, explaining their low survival rate.

As the Middle Ages transitioned into the Renaissance, many toys were homemade and mirrored life, such as dolls, figures of saints, horses, and knights. Large fairs might feature a merchant or two selling trinkets for children.

Members of the aristocracy ordered toys, often made of precious metals, from skilled silversmiths and other masters. As the period ended, adults, especially women, began to collect miniature rooms, which were exact duplicates to scale of larger rooms. Cabinets of curiosities, which included old toys, were in vogue by the seventeenth century.

European Toys of the Seventeenth, Eighteenth, and Nineteenth Centuries

As early as the fifteenth century, Nuremberg, Germany, established itself as the European toy capital. Manufacturing toys became a major cottage industry. Carved wooden toys were given to agents

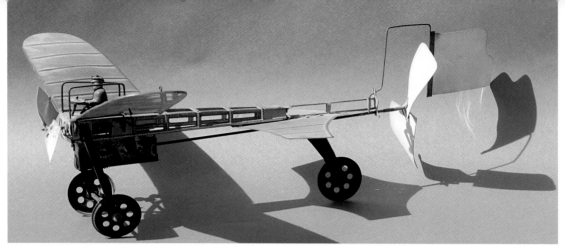

The possibility of flight fascinated young boys as well as their fathers in the early decades of the twentieth century. Märklin produced this articulated, painted tin airplane around 1910.

to be sold at markets and fairs. Families concentrated on making one or two types of toys, often for several generations. By the late 1700s, cottage manufacturers were creating toys made of cardboard, leather, paper, silver, tinplate, and wood.

By the beginning of the nineteenth century, the German toy cottage industry was rapidly fading. New innovations in manufacturing techniques like iron casting, and new materials like papier-mâché and tinplate, opened the door to the mass-production of toys. German and other European manufacturers perfected the hand-painted and lithographed tin wind-up toy. Stamped tin gears replaced heavier and more awkward brass gears. Trains, trolleys, and other toys became a whirlwind of motion. Leading German manufacturers included Gebrüder Bing (Nuremberg, 1866–1933), Georges Carette et CIE (Nuremberg, 1886–1917), Lehmann (Brandenberg, 1881, acquired by VEB Mechanische Spielwaren in 1948), Märklin (Göppingen, Germany, founded in 1859), and Schuco (Nuremberg, 1912–1976). By 1900 a third of all the toys sold in the United States were imported from Germany.

The mass-production of dolls also began in the late nineteenth century. Some firms made dolls as well as doll heads and parts which they sold to other manufacturers. The end of the nineteenth century also witnessed the advent of the stuffed and plush toy. Leading manufacturers include:

- Bru Jeune et CIE (Paris, France, 1866–1899)
- Chad Valley (Birmingham, England, 1897–1978)
- Dean's Rag Book Co., Ltd. (London and South Wales, England, founded in 1903)
- J. K. Farnell (London, England, 1840–1968)
- Heinrich Handwerk (Walterhausen, Germany, 1876–1932)
- Herman (Sonneberg, Germany, founded 1907)
- Jumeau (Montreuil, France, 1842–1899)
- Kämmer & Reinhardt (Walterhausen, Germany, 1886–1930)
- Kestner & Co. (Walterhausen, Germany, 1805–1938)
- Käthe Kruse Doll Company (Donauwörth, Germany, founded 1911)

- Lenci (Turin, Italy, 1919)
- Merrythought Ltd. (Ironbridge, England, founded 1919)
- Simon & Halbig (Gräfenhain, 1869–1920)
- Margarette Steiff GmbH (Giegen, Germany, founded in 1880).

Christmas was the great Victorian contribution to the toy community. Queen Victoria, introduced to the holiday celebration by Prince Albert, promoted the holiday. Christmas's role as a time of gift-giving was firmly established by the mid-nineteenth century, and pictures of Christmas trees with gifts under them and toy train platforms date from the 1880s.

Toys in America

Prior to the arrival of Europeans, Native American children played with leather balls stuffed with feathers, miniature bows and arrows, and cornhusk dolls. Members of the 1585 Roanoke Expedition carried dolls dressed in Elizabethan costume,

Armand Marseille, one of the most prolific doll manufacturers of the first third of the twentieth century, made this 24-inch high, bisque socket head, composition Queen Louise doll.

What's in the Middle?

Joshua Cowen, born August 15, 1877, began his career working for the Acme Electric Lamp Company in Manhattan. It was the golden age of electricity. Cowan was responsible for creating variations of battery-operated lamps.

In 1901 he was asked to create a special window display. His response was "Electric Express," a display featuring a train that drew its power from a dry cell battery attached to the track. It was a huge hit. Orders for similar displays flowed in.

In 1903 Joshua Cowen organized the Lionel Manufacturing Company to produce window displays of electric trains and trolleys. Within five years, the company began marketing its toy trains and trolleys as toys. The rest is history.

Where did the name Lionel originate? It was Joshua Cowen's middle name.

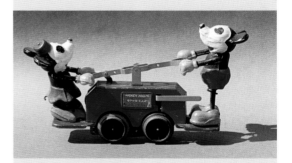

The Mickey and Minnie Lionel side car first appeared in the company's 1935 catalog. The period box adds approximately 20 percent to the value of the toy. Four color variations of the base—apple green, maroon, orange, and red—are known.

The Noah's ark toy has been a popular toy for centuries. In the 1970s, ARCO, a gasoline company, offered a plastic Noah's ark, Noah and his wife, and thirty animal pairs as promotional premiums.

dren had more leisure time. They enjoyed toys, such as dolls, imported from Europe.

A doll brought from Europe to Pennsylvania in 1699 is acknowledged by doll collectors as the oldest surviving doll in the United States. It is known as "Letitia Penn," named after the daughter of William Penn. Many Pennsylvania German farmers, who could not buy such imports, instead whittled toys for their children. The Letitia Penn doll currently resides in the Historical Society of Pennsylvania Collection at the Atwater Kent Museum of Philadelphia.

Benjamin Franklin chronicled the existence of a toy store in Boston as early as 1713, where whistles were sold for a few coppers. The Lottery of the Pious or Spiritual Treasure Casket, an early board game, was printed in America in 1744.

The Philadelphia *Independent Gazette* featured a 1785 advertisement from a merchant selling dolls,

which they gave to the children they found in the New World.

The first American toys

During the colonization of North America, childhood play was discouraged in some regions —especially Puritan New England. Children were considered miniature adults, often expected to work beside their parents at a very young age. When a child was allowed to play with a toy, it was usually on Sunday and then only if the toy taught a moral lesson. A Noah's Ark is a good example. In spite of these restrictions, children created their own toys from available materials, such as making dolls from corncobs. Perhaps because of the use of slave labor, free Southern chil-

R. Bliss Manufacturing Company, known primarily for its wooden and lithograph paper dollhouses, also made this 1882 reissue *Ocean Wave* wood and lithograph paper sailing ship.

J. & E. Stevens, Cromwell, Connecticut, first produced the Eagle and Eaglets mechanical bank in 1883. The coin is placed in the eagle's beak. When the lever is pressed, the eaglets pop up and the eagle tilts forward and drops the coin into the nest.

drums, and toy harps. These stores were stocked primarily with imported European toys, most of which were German in origin. Catalogs and price lists sent directly to the customer arrived on the scene as the eighteenth century ended.

Early nineteenth-century toys

Paper toys were among the earliest mass-produced toys in the United States. R. Bliss Manufacturing Company (Pawtucket, Rhode Island, 1832–1914), Charles M. Crandall (Covington, Pennsylvania, 1820–1905), Gibbs Manufacturing Company (Canton, Ohio, 1884–1969), and W. S. Reed Toy Company (Leominster, Massachusetts, 1875–1897) were pioneers in the manufacture of lithograph paper on wood toys. Gibbs survived longest because they had the foresight to switch from paper to lithograph tin toys.

The ready availability of cast-iron and tin by the early 1850s resulted in a number of American manufacturers turning their focus to the production of toys. American manufacturers began to answer the growing demand for affordable and readily available toys.

John and Elisha Stevens founded J. & E. Stevens (Cromwell, Connecticut) in 1843. The company's cast-iron "Fire Cracker Pistol" appeared in 1859. By the 1870s, the company introduced a line of mechanical banks. Kyser & Rex (Philadelphia, Pennsylvania, 1880–1884), Pratt & Letchworth (Buffalo, New York, 1880s–1900), and Shepard Hardware Company (Buffalo, New York, 1866–1892) are cast-iron manufacturers whose production was limited to the nineteenth century.

Tin plate is made by dipping thin layers of iron or steel in molten tin. The earliest tin toys date from the

Games Go to War: Civil War Games

Playing card manufacturers made a fortune during the Civil War. Card games, often used for gambling, were very popular. Monte, a popular card game during the Mexican American War, was played in a two- and four-card format. Faro also utilized a deck of cards.

In 1863, a Union colonel attempting to smuggle contraband was caught on the road between Alexandria and Fairfax Court House, Virginia, with 4,000 packs of playing cards. It was not unusual for the cargo of British blockade runners to include English manufactured card decks with Confederate themes.

Milton Bradley, a Springfield, Massachusetts, lithographer, introduced "The Checkered Game of Life" in 1860. When the Civil War broke out, Bradley produced a small travel kit of games, which he billed as "Games for Soldiers." The kit contained nine games including backgammon, checkers, and his own The Checkered Game of Life. By the late 1860s, the Milton Bradley Company catalog included dissected maps and puzzles as well as games.

1840s. By the 1850s, Philadelphia was one of the leading centers for the manufacture of tin toys. The Philadelphia Tin Toy Manufactory/Francis, Field & Francis (1838–1850s) made clockwork, pull, and stationary toys. James Fallows & Sons (1874–1890s) also would locate there. Other early tin toy manufacturers were Althof Bergmann & Company (New York, New York, 1867–1880) and George Brown (Forestville, Connecticut, 1856–1880).

F.A.O. Schwarz, America's leading toy store, opened its doors for business in 1862. It continues to serve as a barometer for the best in toy design to this day.

Late nineteenth-century and early twentieth-century toys

The American industrial revolution was well underway by the time of the Civil War, 1861–1865. American ingenuity and genius made the country a worldwide leader in mass-production technology by the end of the nineteenth century.

Cast-iron toys appeared in greater and greater quantity as the nineteenth century neared its end. Mechanical banks, still banks, cap pistols, horse-drawn circus wagons, fire engines, trains, and a host of other types of vehicles filled America's toy shops and the pages of mail-order catalogs. Many cast-iron manufacturers that began in the nineteenth century survived well into the twentieth. Examples include :

- Arcade Manufacturing Company (Freeport, Illinois, 1885–1946)
- Dent Hardware Company (Fullerton, Pennsylvania, 1895–1937)
- Gong Bell Manufacturing Company (East Hampton, Connecticut, 1866–1960s)
- Hubley Manufacturing Company (Lancaster, Pennsylvania, founded in 1894)
- E. R. Ives & Company (Bridgeport, Connecticut, 1862–1932)
- Kenton Hardware Company (Kenton, Ohio, 1890–1953)
- J & E Stevens Company (Cromwell, Connecticut, 1843–1930s)
- Wilkins Toy Company (Keene, New Hampshire, 1880–1919).

In response to the renewed interest in cast-iron toys following World War I, two new manufacturers entered the marketplace:

- Kilgore Manufacturing Company (Westerville, Ohio, 1925–1978)
- Kingsbury Manufacturing Company (Keene, New Hampshire, 1919–1942).

E. R. Ives & Company, Bridgeport, CT, manufactured this cast-iron, horse-drawn, articulated pumper around 1900. It was one of several pieces of horse-drawn fire equipment in the Ives line.

 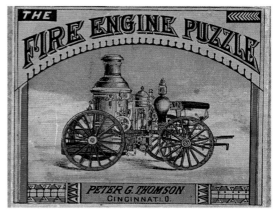

LEFT: George McManus's *Bringing Up Father* cartoon strip featuring Jiggs, Maggie, daughter Nora, and tavern wonder Dinty Moore first appeared in syndication on January 12, 1913. The figures date from the 1930s. RIGHT: Peter G. Thomson, Cincinnati, Ohio, produced puzzles in the 1880s. His Fire Engine Puzzle competed with Milton Bradley's Fire Department Puzzle and McLoughlin Brothers' Fire-Engine Scroll Puzzle.

The toy train reached maturity during this period. Leading manufacturers were American Flyer (Chicago, Illinois, 1907–1966), Hafner Manufacturing Company (Chicago, Illinois, 1900–1950), Lionel Manufacturing Company (New York, New York, 1903–1969), E. R. Ives & Company and Louis Marx and Company (New York, New York, 1921–1976).

Several American toy manufacturers began as wholesalers of European toys. Louis Marx and Company is an example. George Borgfeldt & Company (New York, New York, 1881–1920s) pioneered toy licensing and wholesale importing.

Boxed board and card games enjoyed enormous popularity immediately following the Civil War. Many manufacturers also were engaged in publishing children's books and other materials. Milton Bradley (Springfield, Massachusetts, founded 1861), McLoughlin Brothers (New York, New York, 1828–1920), and Parker Brothers (Salem, Massachusetts, founded 1883) are the three best-known.

Although commonly associated with toy products made in the post-World War I era, the Daisy Manufacturing Company (Plymouth, Michigan, founded 1888) and Tinkertoy (Evanston, Illinois, founded 1915) actually predate the war.

The importance of World War I

Prior to World War I, toys in the United States had been made domestically or imported from Europe. During the war, importation of German-made toys was virtually eliminated and the flow of toys from other countries was greatly reduced. American toy manufacturers rose to the occasion, expanding the range and quantity of toy production. When World War I ended, American toy manufacturers controlled the domestic market.

American dominance of the toy market

Although Germany resumed the exportation of its toys following World War I, it never regained its pre-war market share. The 1920s and first half of

How an Automobile Fender Resulted in a Line of Toys

In 1910 Fred A. Lundahl founded the Moline Pressed Steel Company, located in Moline, Illinois, to manufacture fenders for International Harvester trucks. In 1916, Fred and his wife had a son who they named Buddy.

When Buddy turned four in 1920, Fred decided to make a pressed-steel, scaled down version of the full-size International Harvester open-bed pickup truck for which he supplied fenders. Buddy was thrilled. So were his playmates. Noting this, Lundahl developed a pressed steel toy steam shovel and line of toy trucks. He contacted toy buyers at F.A.O. Schwarz and Marshall Field & Co. Both placed large orders for the 1921 Christmas season.

What should Fred Lundahl call his new line of toys? The answer was simple—Buddy L.

the 1930s belonged to American manufactured toys. Almost their entire production was sold within the United States.

Cast-iron, pressed-steel, and lithograph-tin toys dominated this era. The design of toy airplanes, automobiles, boats, tractors, and trains mirrored the actual vehicles from which they were copied.

Pressed-steel toy giants include:

- Buddy L (Moline, Illinois, 1910–1939)
- Girard Manufacturing Company (Girard, Pennsylvania, 1919–1935)
- Keystone Manufacturing Company (Boston, Massachusetts, 1925–1957)
- Metalcraft Corporation (St. Louis, Missouri, 1920s–1940s)
- Steelcraft (J. W. Murray Manufacturing Company, Cleveland, Ohio, 1920s–1940s)

- Structo Manufacturing Company, (Freeport, Illinois, 1908–1975)
- Wolverine Supply & Manufacturing (Pittsburg, Pennsylvania 1903–1950s)

Some of the many lithograph tin toy manufacturers and wholesalers are:

- Wyandotte Toys (All Metal Products Company, Wyandotte Michigan, 1920–1956)
- Chein & Company (Harrison, New Jersey, 1903–1979)
- Louis Marx & Company (New York, New York, 1919–1979)
- Ohio Art (Bryan, Ohio, founded 1908)
- Strauss Manufacturing Corporation (New York, New York, 1900s–1940s)
- Tootsietoy (Chicago, Illinois, 1876–1961)

Materials such as composition—a mixture of pulp, sawdust, and wood chips mixed with glue and pressed—celluloid, and rubber expanded the toy

Squeaky the Clown, #777, with bobbing head that squeaked joined Fisher-Price's line in 1958. It remained in production for two years. It was reissued as a ToyFest toy in 1995.

LEFT: The Alexander Doll Company enjoyed a loyal following throughout the 20th century. Alexander introduced its Alexanderkins, also known as "Wendykins," in 1953.
RIGHT: Girls who grew up in the first two decades following the end of World War II were likely to own one or more more Ideal Toy & Novelty Company dolls, such as this 1949-1953 Toni doll.

material vocabulary. Auburn and Sun Rubber were two leading manufacturers of rubber toy vehicles.

Several specialized toy companies, such as Duncan (Los Angeles, California, founded 1928), Fisher-Price (East Aurora, New York, founded 1930), and Lincoln Logs (Chicago, Illinois, founded 1920), also date from this period. The Ingersoll Watch Company (New York, New York, 1880–1944) produced character watches begin-ning in the early 1930s. U.S. Time entered the market in the post-1945 period.

Although several American teddy bear, doll, and plush toy manufacturers predate World War I, they enjoyed a period of prosperity and growth in the 1920s and early 1930s. These include:

- Alexander Doll Company (New York, New York, founded 1923)
- Character Toy and Novelty Company (South Norwalk, Connecticut, late 1920s–1983)
- Martha Jenks Chase (Rhode Island, 1889–late 1930s or early 1940s)
- Effanbee (New York, New York, founded 1910)
- Georgene Novelties Company (New York, New York, 1920–1962)
- Gund (Edison, New Jersey, founded 1898)
- E. I. Horsman & Company (New York, New York, founded 1865)

Louis Marx & Company introduced its lithograph tin, Merrymakers mouse band in the early 1930s. There are four variations of this toy. The violinist with the backdrop is the most desirable.

Although designed primarily for play by young boys, Wm. Britain's Armies of the World sets quickly became popular with adult collectors who incorporated them into battlefield dioramas.

include Barclay Manufacturing Company (Hoboken, New Jersey, 1923–1971), William Britain LTD (London, England, founded in 1845), and Manoil Manufacturing Company, Inc. (Waverly, New York, 1927–1955).

As the 1930s ended, American toy manufacturers began exporting toys abroad, especially to Europe. At the same time, inexpensive Japanese-made toys, especially lithograph tin toys, were introduced to the American market.

- Ideal Toy & Novelty Company (Brooklyn, New York, founded 1903)
- Knickerbocker Toy Company (New York, New York, 1920s–1960s)
- A. Schoenhut Company (Philadelphia, Pennsylvania, 1872–1935).

Toys soldiers gained in popularity. American manufacturers specialized in inexpensive dime store soldiers. Higher-end soldiers were made by foreign manufacturers. The most important manufacturers

The importance of World War II

As America went to war from 1941 to 1945, most toy manufacturers retooled their plants to produce war supplies. Materials, especially metals, used to make toys were needed for military goods. Instead, the toys manufactured during this period were made of pressed cardboard or wood.

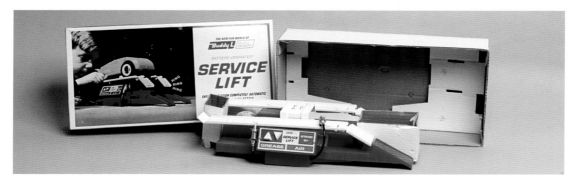

Buddy L, known primarily for its pressed-steel products, began manufacturing toys in plastics in the mid-1960s. This battery-operated service lift with its magnetic action nozzle is copyrighted 1967.

The Post-1945 Era

America emerged from World War II as an industrial giant. New advances in materials, technology, and production were redirected to creating inexpensive, mass-produced domestic goods. New toy introductions increased dramatically from pre-war statistics.

Pressed-steel and lithograph tin toys competed with die-cast and plastic toys. By the early 1960s, die-cast and plastic toys dominated. Improvements in injection molding led to the 1959 introduction of Barbie and the action figures of the 1960s.

European and Japanese manufacturers reentered the toy arena with a vengeance in the twenty years following World War II. Initially, Japan flooded the market with a wealth of battery-operated, friction, and wind-up lithograph tin toys. The Swedish Lego and British Matchbox became prominent players in the American marketplace.

The 1950s and 1960s were a golden age for American toy manufacturers. Pre-war firms such as A. C. Gilbert and Marx continued to grow. Many new privately owned firms flourished. Hasbro, founded in 1923 by Henry and Helal Hassenfeld, began a slow growth process that would turn it, along with Harold "Matt" Matson and Elliott Handler's Mattel, into one of the Big Two toy companies of the twenty-first century.

One factor which greatly changed the American toy industry in the late

ABOVE: The Vernon Company of Newton, Iowa, issued this Blackout Kit in 1942. It included an instruction booklet entitled "Hundreds of uses for Blackout Kutouts: The New Wonder Material/Glows in the Dark." BELOW: Louis Marx Playsets ranging from medieval castles to western towns and stockades were extremely popular in the 1960s and early 1970s. Because of the large number of pieces, it is difficult to find complete examples. Period boxes are even scarcer.

Many battery-operated toy vehicles featured hand controls that allowed the children to drive them across the room and throughout the house.

1960s and 1970s was product safety requirements. New child safety laws altered designs and materials, especially in toys for babies and children under age three. Toys affected by the new safety awareness included anything that might be flammable, contain lead, have sharp edges, or present a choking hazard.

By the end of the 1960s more and more American toy manufacturers were moving their production facilities offshore and even Barbie was manufactured in Japan. In the 1970s Hong Kong replaced Japan as the major manufacturer of plastic toys. By the mid-1980s, production was shifting from Hong Kong to China. Today, the vast majority of "American" toys are made in China.

In the early 1970s, acquisition fever ran rampant. Many toy firms were purchased by large conglomerates. Many of these conglomerates were purchased and merged with other conglomerates. As foreign competition—especially from

Milton Bradley first issued Battleship as a paper and pencil game in 1931. Milton Bradley was marketing a plastic version by the 1970s. Thanks to its acquisition of Milton Bradley, Battleship is today a Hasbro product.

This 1979 Matchbox Construction Set, G-5, contains a Loadavator for loading rocks, sand, and gravel; a dump truck; a cement mixer; a bulldozer; a shovel-nose tractor; and a Bomag road roller. Beginning in the late 1970s Matchbox created assortments of vehicles grouped by common theme as a method of increasing sales.

Asia—grew, many of the toy acquisitions failed to meet corporate financial projections. Toy divisions were closed or sold. In 1963 General Mills bought Parker Brothers. It was then sold to Kenner, which was acquired by Tonka. When Hasbro bought Tonka in 1991, it acquired the rights to Parker Brothers. Having acquired Milton Bradley in 1984, Hasbro now has virtual control of the boxed board-game marketplace.

As the twenty-first century dawned, two American toy manufacturers, Hasbro and Mattel, dominated the global toy market. Some foreign manufacturers, such as Lego, have captured niche markets. However, at the moment, there appears to be no challenger to Hasbro and Mattel.

To illustrate the extent to which smaller companies have been bought up and merged, Hasbro's subsidiaries now include Avalon Hill, Coleco, Galoob, Kenner, Maisto, Milton Bradley, Parker Brothers, Playskool, Selchow and Righter, Tiger Electronic, Tonka, Wizards of the Coast, and Wrebbit. Fisher-Price, Hot Wheels, Matchbox, and View-Master are among Mattel's many subsidiaries. Hasbro produces more than twenty branded toys, among which are Action Man, Easy Bake Oven, G.I. Joe, Lincoln Logs, Lite-Brite, Mr.

Potato Head, My Little Pony, Play-Doh, Spirograph, Tinkertoys, and Transformers.

The electronic toy era

The electronic toy arrived on the scene in the mid-1980s. In less than twenty years, the electronic toy has become dominant in the teenage toy marketplace. In fact, its dominance has led to the designation of today's youngsters as the "single digit" toy generation—in other words, non-electronic toys are primarily designed and sold to infants and children under the age of ten.

Atari introduced Pong as a coin-operated video game on November 29, 1972. The Pong home console was first demonstrated at the Consumer Electronics Show in the summer of 1975. Sears, Roebuck and Company ordered 75,000 units. Pong's success was ensured.

CHAPTER TWO

BEGINNING A COLLECTION

Every toy you acquire should tempt you to play with it. Occasionally, actually more often than not, yield to this temptation. If you find yourself taking collecting too seriously, let fun and play be reminders of why you chose this hobby.

The number of ways in which toys can be collected is unlimited—you can choose them by category, chronology, country of origin or region, manufacturer, type, or a host of other ways. It is unlikely that a collector will ever be able to own one of every example known. Even if your funds and time were unlimited, no collector could accomplish this in one lifetime. There are simply too many toys out there.

Develop a Collecting Philosophy

A collecting philosophy is a set of guidelines that helps you focus your collecting efforts. It maximizes your time and spending, and enhances your ability to display what you acquire. In modern terms, it is a strategic plan to manage your collection.

"He who dies with the biggest pile wins" is not a wise collecting philosophy. A collecting philosophy usually consists of no more than three or four sentences. It is better to be too broad than

OPPOSITE: Rock 'em Sock 'em Robots.

Magic Lanterns, mostly Germany in origin, were the first children's slide projectors. Because of their scarcity, a collection in excess of twenty-five units is considered a large collection.

too narrow at first. There are some key considerations you should be mindful of in developing a collecting philosophy.

1. Collecting approach
2. Time available to devote to the hunt and documenting the collection
3. Amount of disposable income
4. Space, both for display and storage
5. Availability of objects
6. Condition parameters
7. Time period
8. Security

Sample collecting philosophy #1: broad approach

I am going to build a collection of television cowboy show toys licensed between the late 1940s and 1980. I will focus on toys that are complete, in their period box (when applicable), and in very good or better condition. I plan to display 70 percent or more of the toys I buy in my home and business office. I also plan to build a reference database.

Sample collecting philosophy #2: narrow approach

I am going to assemble a full set of Holiday Barbies in their period boxes. Each example will be between C9 and C10 condition. The collection will include examples marketed in the United States as well as abroad. I also will create a research database.

A collecting philosophy is not absolute: When a revision is necessary, make it. Adjustments, even a major change of focus, in your collecting philosophy are very much a part of your evolution into a toy connoisseur. Expect to learn from your collecting experiences.

The television cowboy Western dominated the viewing screen during the 1950s. *The Life and Legend of Wyatt Earp*, starring Hugh O'Brian, aired on ABC from September 6, 1955, to September 26, 1961.

Manufacturers often produced the same toy in different sizes and paint schemes. Collectors often try to assemble all known variants of a single toy, displaying them in such a fashion to illustrate the differences as with this collection of Arcade cast-iron taxis.

Collecting by Category

Most toy collectors begin collecting using a category approach. As they become more sophisticated, they often develop specialized collections within that category. It's important to narrow your collecting focus before you begin collecting. Narrowing your choice is not going to be easy as you are most certainly going to be tempted by more than one category.

You can adopt a multi-category approach initially. However, a good general rule is the more diverse a toy collection, the less meaningful. The unique identity and character of your toy collection should be established by your tenth acquisition.

What follows are a number of basic toy categories. Each category contains three types of information: how toy collectors approach the category, collecting hints, and collectors' clubs. The information can be supplemented by reading more on each subject and continuing field education. More than a dozen specialized reference titles are available for many categories. (Since specialized reference titles often remain in print only for a short time you may have to find them online. Two of the best websites to locate valuable out-of-print titles are www.abebooks.com and www.bookfinder.com.)

Action figures

Action figures is a generic term for a group of male-oriented, fully-articulated plastic figures that arrived on the toy scene in the mid-1960s. Hasbro's G.I. Joe, which was released in 1964, is credited with initiating the action figure craze.

The action figure replaced the toy vehicle as the dominant boys toy by the mid-1970s and has not relinquished its market position even though its popularity has waned somewhat in the twenty-first

Collectors prefer action figures still in their period blister packs, as is this See-Threepio (C-3PO) example. Kenner issued the first *Star Wars* action figures in 1977.

century. Action figures are sold globally, albeit occasionally with a different marketing emphasis, for example G.I. Joe is known as Action Man in Europe.

Action figures are meant to be posed, and for that reason have moveable joints. They often are accompanied by a wealth of accessory equipment including costumes and vehicles. Action figures range in size from 3 3⁄4" to more than 12".

They can depict a wide variety of being such as aliens, humans, or superheroes. Human figures range from real-life personalities, including a wealth of sports heroes, to cartoon, movie, television, and video game characters. Ideal's Captain Action (1966-1968), Mattel's Major Matt Mason (1967-70), and Marx's Best of the West (1965-1975) are favored by older collectors. Younger collectors focus on series from Hasbro, Kenner, and McFarlane. Some characters, Batman and Superman, appeal universally to all generations of collectors.

Action figures have their greatest value when still in their period blister packs. Since the same figure may appear in several different series, collectors track the issues by the information found on the back of the blister pack.

Collectors' Clubs: Official G.I. Joe Collectors Club (225 Cattle Baron Parc Drive, Fort Worth, TX 76108; www.gijoeclub.com); International G.I. Joe Collectors Club (150 South Glenoaks Boulevard, Burbank, CA 91510; www.gijoeinformation.com); G.I. Joe: Steel Brigade Command (8362 Lomary Avenue, Westminster, CA 96283; www.steelbridgade.com); TransMasters (1215 South Andrews Road, Yorktown, IN 47396).

Banks

Banks divide into two basic groups, mechanical (or action) and still (or no action). There are semi-mechanical banks, banks in which a bell rings when the coin is deposited or ones that register the amount in the bank. These attract the interest of only a very small number of collectors.

American collectors prefer American-made cast-iron, mechanical banks from firms such as Kyser & Rex Co. of Frankford, PA, Shepard Hardware Co. of Buffalo, NY, and J. & E. Stevens Co. of Cromwell, CT. In addition to cast iron, mechanical banks were made from cardboard, tin, lead, papier mâché, white metal, and wood.

Since the 1970s, mechanical banks have been considered one of the blue chip toy investment categories. Prices for the most desirable examples now exceed $100,000. Because of their age, investment quality begins at the relatively low fine condition, and condition is partly based on the amount of surviving period paint. Value is exponential, with the

J. & E. Stevens manufactured the Darktown Battery Bank. The pitcher tosses the coin. As the batter swings, the catcher drops and the coin enters the bank. Because mechanical banks were used, it is difficult to find examples with 75 percent or more of period paint.

greatest increases in price when surviving paint reaches 90 percent plus.

In addition to original toys, mechanical banks have been reproduced since the 1920s. Although most reproductions are easily identified, some of the early examples are hard to distinguish from originals.

Normally, collectors think of still banks in terms of late nineteenth and early-twentieth century cast-iron examples, but wonderful collections can also be built by focusing on lithograph tin and plastic banks. The number of still banks is extremely large, so many collectors choose a specific theme.

Collectors' Clubs: Mechanical Bank Collectors of America (PO Box 13323, Pittsburgh, PA 15234; www.mechanicalbanks.org); Still Bank Collectors Club of America (4175 Millersville, Road, Indianapolis, IN 46205).

Battery-operated toys

The Japanese introduced the battery-operated toy to the world in the fifteen-year period following the end of World War II. Previously, American and European manufacturers only used batteries to add realism, for instance, causing the headlights on a toy automobile to shine.

From 1945 through the late 1960s was the golden age of the battery-operated toy. Most examples were lithograph tin. Examples ranged from automata—such as Charlie Weaver the Bartender or Barber Bear—to a full range of vehicles. Robots and space vehicles entered the battery-operated scene in the late 1960s.

Major manufacturers include Alps, Ashai Toy, Bandai, Linemar (Marx's Japanese subsidiary), Marusan, Marx, Toy Nomura, and Yonezawa.

Japanese-produced battery-operated toys flooded the American market in the 1950s and 1960s. Many of these, such as this bartender, appealed to adults as well as children. Most boxes contained wonderful colored illustrations of the toy. Hence, they must be present for the toy to be complete.

Many of these toys came in boxes with colorful and highly decorative artwork. In some cases, the value of the period box may exceed the value of the toy.

Battery-operated toys, especially those of German and Japanese origin, are highly sought after in the global marketplace. American collectors constantly find themselves competing with foreign collectors.

Board games

Boxed board games divide into distinct chronological periods: (1) late nineteenth century to 1920; (2) 1920 to 1940: (3) 1945-1980; and (4) post-1980. Milton Bradley, McLoughlin Brothers, and Parker Brothers games dominate the first period. Game boxes often feature highly colorful, elaborate lithographed covers. Following the end of World

LEFT: J. H. Singer, New York, New York, was primarily a producer of games and novelties from the mid-1880s through the mid-1890s. This "Telegraph Messenger" game, circa 1890, is collected primarily for its colorful lithograph cover. RIGHT: *Have Gun, Will Travel*, starring Richard Boone as Paladin, aired on CBS from September 14, 1957, through September 21, 1963. This Parker Brothers game is copyrighted 1959.

War I, many new manufacturers entered the boxed board game marketplace, and the quality of the games suffered. Cover artwork lacked the pizzazz of the earlier period. During this period, the licensing of boxed board games began. Newspaper cartoons provided the first licenses. A limited number of personality licenses, such as a Babe Ruth baseball game, were also granted.

From 1945 to 1980 was the golden age of the boxed board game. Television licensing dominated: Almost every television Western series had its own boxed board game. As the period ended, movie licensing challenged and eventually replaced television licensing as the driving marketing force.

Limited licensing continued into the post-1980 period. Hasbro acquired Parker Brothers and even-

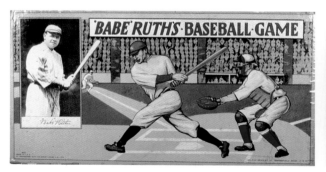

LEFT: Milton Bradley manufactured this " 'Babe' Ruth's Baseball Game" in the mid-1920s when the Sultan of Swat was nearing the peak of his career. RIGHT: Parker Brothers licensed and first manufactured Monopoly in 1935. Since then, millions of sets have been sold worldwide. Thousands of variations, many used for local fundraisers, are known.

tually Milton Bradley. Generic games such as Candy Land, Monopoly, and Scrabble became the focus of sales. A generic game is a general game that has continued in production for decades. Battleship, Monopoly, Parcheesi, and Tiddly Winks are examples.

A complete game has its game board, all its playing pieces, instructions, and box. Pieces frequently get misplaced or lost in play. Carefully check any boxed board game before purchasing it.

Collectors' Club: Association of Game and Puzzle Collectors, (197M Boston Post Road West, Marlborough, MA 01752; www.agpc.org).

Cast-iron

Cast-iron was first used to produce toys in the 1870s. A prototype of the toy was made. It was then broken down into a series of parts, each of which was used to create the mold used for sand casting. After the parts were molded, they were cooled, cleaned, filed, and assembled to make the toy. The cast-iron toy age ended at the start of World War II. However, a few companies, for

Motorcycle toys became a hot collectibles in the mid-1990s. This Hubley cast-iron police motorcycle dates from the 1930s.

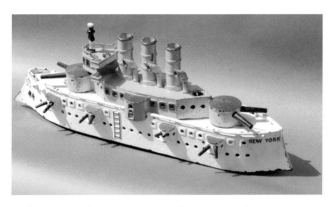

The Dent Hardware Company, Fullerton, Pennsylvania, is known primarily for its cast-iron cars and trucks. However, the pièce de résistance for Dent collectors is this cast-iron battleship from the 1920s.

example, Ertl, continued to make cast-iron toys in the post-1945 period.

Most cast-iron toys are found in type collections—for instance, collections of banks, circus, farm toys, horse-drawn wagons, guns, toy soldiers, or vehicles. Collecting by company, such as Arcade, Hubley, Kenton, etc., is another approach.

Collecting chronologically, for example pre-1919 or 1920s/30s, or concentrating on examples manufactured in a small geographic region, for instance central Connecticut or eastern Pennsylvania, are other ways to collect cast-iron toys.

Originality and period paint are collecting keys. Since cast-iron toys rust, collectors frequently encounter repainted examples.

Celluloid

Celluloid, created from nitrocellulose, camphor, dyes, and other agents, is generally acknowledged to be the first thermoplastic. Created in 1856, it was originally known as Parkesine. The term "celluloid" was not used until 1870.

This Japanese celluloid toy dates from the 1930s. Exposing celluloid toys to rapid changes in temperature may cause them to crack. Because the celluloid is often thin, excessive pressure can cause an indentation.

Celluloid was used for doll faces and figures on lithograph tin windup toys. Toy collectors define a celluloid toy as one made completely from celluloid.

Celluloid was a popular material used to make Christmas and other holiday toys. Celluloid Christmas Santas, Easter rabbits, and Halloween figures dating from the pre-World War I era and the 1920s and 1930s are eagerly sought by holiday collectors.

Celluloid discolors over time and is easily damaged through handling and heat. Damaged examples are nearly impossible to repair.

Character/licensed toys

Most character collectors specialize. There are numerous possibilities from television series—everything from Westerns to music groups such as the Beatles or Kiss. This category also includes many characters and personalities from cartoons, comic books, comic strips, movies, radio, sports, stage, television, and video games. The more popular the figure, the greater the number of toys licensed. The more toys produced, the greater the survival rate. However, what is common in the United

The Origin of the Licensed Toy

When one thinks of a toy, one thinks of the inventor, manufacturer, or child who plays with it. Little or no thought is given to the toy wholesaler or jobber. George Borgfeldt & Company (1881–1962), New York, New York, originated the concept of the licensed toy. Brothers George and Marshal Borgfeldt and Joseph Kahle founded the wholesale importing company.

In the late 1920s, Borgfeldt acquired the rights to produce toys based on famous cartoon characters and strips of the day—Barney Google and Spark Plug, Felix the Cat, Maggie & Jiggs, and Toonerville Trolley. A Disney license followed.

How do you identify a Borgfeldt licensed toy? Look for the company's "Nifty" logo, a smiling moon face.

Fontaine Fox created the Toonerville Trolley comic strip in 1908 for the *Chicago Post*. It began nationally syndicated in 1918. The cast included a bunch of eccentric characters including Mickey (Himself) McGuire, Skipper and his Trolley, and Powerful Katrinka.

Revell manufactured a model kit for each of the four Beatles in 1965. The Lennon kit is stock number 1352. The box must be present and the model unassembled for the kit to have full value.

Rocky and His Friends, starring Rocket "Rocky" the Flying Squirrel and Bullwinkle, first appeared as a weekday show on ABC from 1959 to 1960. It was revived as The Bullwinkle Show, airing on NBC from 1961 to 1964. It then moved to ABC, running from 1964 until 1973. These PVC figures of (from left top counter clockwise): Rocky, Natasha Fatale, Dudley Do-Right, Boris Badenov, and Snidely Whiplash date from the late 1960s or early 1970s. Rocky and his friends were the creation of cartoonist Jay Ward.

States is often uncommon abroad, and many characters enjoyed worldwide popularity, creating global demand for some examples.

Many character toys, for example, action figures, board games, puzzles, and vehicles, cross over into other toy collecting categories, thus increasing competition among collectors for the same item.

Collectors' Club: Toonerville Trolley Collectors (4809 Listra Road, Rockville, MD 20853).

Children's toys (pre-school)

This category includes toys used by children from infancy through ages five or six. Most individuals do not remember these toys, however, their parents—especially their mothers—do. As a result, women are the primary collectors of these toys.

Toys manufactured by Fisher-Price and Playskool are the most highly collected pre-school toys. Licensed toys from television shows such as Ding Dong School, Captain Kangaroo, and Sesame Street also are eagerly sought by collectors. Infant toys, from crib toys to rubber squeeze toys, also belong in this category.

Collectors' Club: Fisher-Price Collectors Club (1442 North Ogden, Mesa, AZ 85205; www.fpclub.org).

Fisher-Price introduced Tip Toe Turtle, #773, in 1962. It was produced for eighteen years. It has a solid wood body, polyethylene hat, shell, feet, and legs, and makes a melodious sound when pulled.

LEFT: The A. Schoenhut Company, Philadelphia, Pennsylvania, is known primarily for its pianos, dolls, and circus and other animal playset figures. Schoenhut also made building sets and jigsaw puzzles. Its Little Village Builder contained wooden pieces for a church, schoolhouse, house, railroad station, and freight station. RIGHT: Elgo's American Plastic Bricks were a hit in the late 1940s and early 1950s, successfully challenging Lincoln Logs for market dominance.

Construction toys

Blocks were the first construction toy. Gustav and Otto Lilienthal pioneered the concept of stone building block toys in Germany in the 1870s. However, it was Friedrich A. Richter's Anchor Stone block sets that introduced the concept to a worldwide audience.

Metal, paper, and wooden construction sets followed. A. C. Gilbert introduced its first metal Erector Set in 1913. Tinkertoy was founded in 1915 and Lincoln Logs were invented a year later.

Plastic construction sets gained popularity in the 1950s and 1960s. Lego is today's construction toy equivalent.

It is extremely difficult to find a complete construction toy. Most do not come with a full list of parts. Parts are lost and mismatched over time.

Construction toy licensing is a late 1990s phenomenon. Lego lead the way with its licensing of several *Star Wars, Episode 1: The Phantom Menace* (1999) playsets.

Collectors' Clubs: Anchor Block Foundation (1670 Hawkwood Court, Charlottesville, VA 22901; www.ankerstein.org); A. C. Gilbert Heritage Society (1440 Whalley, Suite 252, New Haven, Connecticut 06515; www.acghs.org)

Die-cast toys

Although die-cast slush metal toys existed prior to World War I, they made their mark in the three decades following the end of World War II. Although inexpensive, they featured great detail and often had moveable parts.

Die-cast vehicles are the second most popular toy, next to action figures, among younger collectors. Most collectors focus on a single company, such as Corgi, Dinky, Hot Wheels, Matchbox, or Tootsietoy.

Because of the large number of issues within these companies, collectors specialize in series and vehicle types. Accessory pieces exist in large quantity, especially for Hot Wheels and Matchbox.

The Aveling Barford Road Roller No. 1 was the first vehicle in the Matchbox I-75 series. Like the earlier Lesney model, the front roller turned. The driver was a new addition.

Accessory sets have almost gained the status of a separate collecting category, much like toy train sets.

Value rests with mint-in-box/package items. Die-cast toys is an expanding category. Brand name categories, e.g., NASCAR collectibles and Winross freight trucks featuring advertising, are two newer examples. Most of these items are purchased by adults and never played with as toys.

The same holds true for collector editions, both from major manufacturers and brand names, some of which are sold at gas stations and specialty outlets.

Collectors' Clubs: Corgi Official Collector Club (PO Box 323, Seanse, SA1 1BJ, United Kingdom); Johnny Lightning Club (3618 Grape Road, Mishawaka, IN 46544; www.playing mantis.com); Matchbox U.S.A. (62 Saw Mill Road, Durham, Connecticut 06422); Matchbox Collectors Club (PO Box 977, Newfield, NJ 08344); Matchbox International Collectors Association (PO Box 120, Deeside, CH5 3HE, United Kingdom; www.matchboxclub.com).

Disneyana/cartoon toys

Disney is king of the hill when it comes to character licensing, and Disneyana is one of the few toy collecting categories where the heart rules over the mind.

Mickey and Minnie Mouse followed by Donald Duck are the most popular Disney cartoon character collectibles. Toys from the earliest Disney feature-length cartoons, such as *Sleeping Beauty* (1959), and *Snow White and the Seven Dwarfs* (1937), *Pinocchio* (1940), and *Alice in Wonderland* (1951) remain desirable. Interest continues to grow for toys from 1950s and 1960s Disney cartoons, such as *Lady and the Tramp* (1955) and *Sleeping Beauty*, television memorabilia, especially Mickey Mouse Club items, and memorabilia associated with Disneyland and Disney World.

Aurora's Model Motoring Stirling Moss Four Lane Racing Set in HO scale, copyrighted 1963, contained four die-cast slot cars.

Walt Disney's animated, full-length classic feature film *Snow White* premiered in December 1937. Film licensing was intense. This *Snow White* kitchen set dates from the early 1960s.

Disney items have global appeal, and many American collectors consider their collections incomplete without foreign examples. For the same reasons, buyers outside the United States eagerly seek American-licensed material. Canada and Europe are ripe markets for material.

Dolls, teddy bears, and plush toys

Doll collectors divide dolls into seven approximate chronological periods:

(1) Eighteenth and early nineteenth century
(2) 1820 to 1880
(3) 1880 to 1915
(4) 1915 to 1940
(5) 1940 to 1959
(6) 1960 to mid-1970s
(7) 1976 to the present.

Traditionalist doll collectors define an antique doll as one made before 1915. These older collectors, whose collecting focus is primarily on late-nineteenth and early twentieth century dolls, are the main constituency of local dolls clubs that comprise the United Federation of Doll Clubs. Collector interest is shifting to post-1945 dolls, as the generations who grew up with Chatty Cathy and Toni want to reacquaint themselves with the dolls of their youth.

Period hair, type of head, fixed or sleep eyes, open or closed mouth, types of hands or feet, body construction, jointed or non-jointed, and period shoes are just a few of the value considerations for pre-1940 dolls. Surprisingly, a period costume accounts for only a small percent of a doll's value.

The middle decades of the twentieth century witnessed a number of major changes in doll manufacture. New materials (plastic), technology (injection molding), and manufacturing location (the Far East) all played a major role in revolutionizing the industry by the mid-1960s. Hard, then soft plastic dolls dominated the market by the mid-1950s.

Barbie arrived on the scene in 1959. The Cabbage Patch doll was the marketing sensation of the 1970s, much as the Bratz doll is today.

The doll industry briefly flirted with soft vinyl, a material touted as providing dolls with the feel of real skin, in the late 1940s. By the early 1950s hard plastic, used to manufacture this Ideal Betsy McCall doll, became the material of choice for mass-market dolls.

Madame Alexander

Beatrice Alexander Behrman (1895–1990), a daughter of Austrian and Russian immigrants, founded the Alexander Doll Company in 1923. Working out of her kitchen with an operating capital of $1,600, Beatrice dubbed herself "Madame Alexander" and developed a cottage industry that produced dolls and doll clothing.

The Alexander Doll Company produced a number of doll "firsts," including marketing baby dolls, using distinctive face molds, manufacturing dolls honoring famous and living individuals, pioneering in the use of hard plastic, and introducing Cissy, the first full-figured haute couture doll. Madame Alexander created an Alice in Wonderland doll in the 1930s and the Scarlett O'Hara doll in 1936.

In the early 1930s, Mildred Alexander, Beatrice's daughter, encouraged her mother to produce a Shirley Temple doll. Madame Alexander passed on the idea, preferring to focus more on dolls associated with literature rather than movies. The Ideal Toy & Novelty Company is eternally grateful.

In 1956, Madame Alexander moved doll production to the former Studebaker automobile plant in Harlem. The company was the last major manufacturer to produce dolls in America.

Where did Beatrice Alexander Behrman develop her interest in dolls? The answer is from working at the Alexander Doll Hospital, located on Grand Street in Manhattan's Lower East Side, operated by Maurice, her father.

This Alexander 17" Maggie from circa 1949–1953 has her "Maggie" wrist tag and box containing metal curlers and net.

The 1980s witnessed the arrival of the collector edition handcrafted dolls, also known as "contemporary" dolls, many of which were and are still being marketed on television home shopping channels. The secondary market for these dolls has not yet been tested.

As collector interest shifts to post-1945 dolls, new collecting criteria, for example, emphasis on having all accessories including tags and literature plus the period box, are being applied. Collectors also have raised their condition expectations, wanting examples in fine or better condition.

Doll manufacturers are quick to copy any successful doll. Horsman's Dorothy looked surprisingly like Effanbee's Patsy doll. Cosmopolitan's Ginger could easily be mistaken for Vogue's Ginny. Take time to familiarize yourself with many different dolls so that you can be certain you know what you are purchasing.

The teddy bear, named for President Theodore Roosevelt, arrived on the scene in late 1902 or early 1903. The Ideal Toy Corporation (American) and Margarette Steiff (German) are among the earliest firms to include a bear in their stuffed toy lines.

Early teddy bears are identified by the humps in

Fulper (1918–1931) made this 25 inch, bisque socket head, composition body doll. The wig has been replaced.

their backs, elongated muzzles, jointed limbs, mohair bodies (with some exceptions), and glass, pin-back, or black shoe button eyes. Stuffing materials include excelsior (the most popular), kapok, and wood-wool. Elongated limbs, over-sized feet, felt paws, and a black embroidered nose and mouth are other indicators of a quality early bear.

The 1980s collector edition handcraft doll movement also spawned a similar interest in con-temporary teddy bears. G. M. Lowenthal and Justina Unger began producing a line of reproduc-tion antiques and duck decoys in 1979. In 1984, the couple issued its first fully-jointed, Merino wool teddy bear in a popular line now known simply as Boyd's Bears. Many individual artisans and small companies entered the marketplace.

The teddy bear is only one of dozens of animals that have been made into plush toys. During the first half of the twentieth century, Ideal and Knickerbocker were just two of the American man-ufacturers who competed against Steiff and other foreign manufacturers. Following World War II, stuffed toys became a favorite prize of carnival games of chance. Most were inexpensive imports from China and Taiwan.

The Beanie Baby is perhaps the best-known plush toy today. The speculative craze that led to its demise became a classic study of a "hot toy bubble."

Collectors' Clubs: Barbie Doll Collectors Club International (PO Box 245, Gar-nerville, NY 10923); Betsey McCall Fan Club (4532 Fertile Valley Road, Newport, WA 99156); Ginny Doll Club (PO Box 756, Oakdale, CA 95361; www.voguedolls.com); Liddle Kiddles Klub (3639 Fourth Avenue, La Crescenta, CA 91214); Strawberry Shortcake Collectors' Club (1409 72nd Street, North Bergen, NJ 07047); United Federation of Doll Clubs (10920 North Ambassador Drive, Suite 130, Kansas City, MO 64153; www.ufdc.org)

Dollhouses and furnishings

There are four key groups of dollhouses: (1) the early lithograph paper on wood dollhouse of the late-nineteenth and early-twentieth century, made by firms such as Bliss Manufacturing Company or Ives; (2) homemade dollhouses from the Victorian period to the present, ranging from the primitive to detailed scaled architectural copies often with inte-rior lighting; (3) lithograph tin dollhouses from the 1920s through the 1960s; and (4) plastic dollhouses from the post-1960 period.

While memory does influence a collector's choice of what type of dollhouse to collect, the romance of earlier eras plays a far greater role. When collectors think of a dollhouse, they usually mean one portraying the Victorian or Edwardian eras, roughly the period from the 1870s through 1919.

Furnishings are sold individually or in sets. Dollhouse furnishings were once a five and dime favorite. Collectors prefer sets in their period boxes,

TOP: Many dollhouses dating from the late nineteenth and early twentieth centuries were homemade, often imitating the house in which the young owner lived. The more elaborate models were made for adult collectors. BELOW: Dollhouse rooms are often decorated with furniture pieces from a variety of different manufacturers and time periods. Only adult collectors insist the pieces in a room are period matched.

which offer a quick method of determining if the set is complete.

Some collectors have no problem mixing and matching furnishings representing different historical forms, shapes, styles, and patterns. Display is more about what looks good rather than what is correct.

Early to mid-twentieth century American manufacturers of dollhouse furnishing include Schoenhut, Tootsietoy, The TynieToy Company, The Toy Furniture Shop of Providence, Rhode Island, Roger Williams Toys, and the Wisconsin Toy Company. These companies faced stiff competition from cheaper Japanese imports. Marx, Petite Princess, Plasco, and Renwal are popular post-1945 American manufacturers.

Dollhouses and furnishings come in a variety of different scales. 1:18, three-quarters of an inch equals one foot, is the most common twentieth century mass-production scale. Marx used a 1:24, one-half inch equals one foot, for its 1950s dollhouses. Beginning in the 1970s, adult collectors began favoring the 1:12 scale, one inch equals one foot. While some collectors have no problem mixing and matching furnishings from different historical forms, miniature collectors are the exception. Many create independent rooms in imitation of nineteenth century collectors where scale and historical accuracy are paramount. The collectors are adults. Furnishings are highly detailed and meant for display, not play.

Educational toys

Collectors make a distinction between children's (pre-school) toys and educational toys. Children's toys are designed primarily for play and directed toward children under the age of five. Educational toys appeal to a broader age group and have a specific educational function.

Educational toys, ranging from the Chautauqua

standing desk to a Fisher-Price computer toy, tend to be used and discarded. Educational toys designed for younger children are developmental. The Tupperware ball-shaped toy is designed to create dexterity as well as teach shape recognition. A bench with pins driven through with a hammer teaches color recognition as well as coordination.

Educational toys for older children are designed to teach social and scientific skills. Children's toy dishes attracted collector interest as early as the 1930s. By the 1970s, they were listed as a major collecting category in most price guide references. Collectors often specialize by material, such as ceramic, glass, or tin, or by manufacturer, such as Akro Agate. Toy collectors prefer to purchase children's dishes as a set in their period box.

A. C. Gilbert pioneered the scientific toy. The Gilbert Science Laboratory introduced many youngsters to the basic principles of chemistry. Educational and scientific toys enjoyed a renaissance at the beginning of the twentieth century. Check out www.fatbrinstoys.com, www.little

Children's block sets serve a variety of functions—helping a child develop motor and coordination skills as well as teaching colors, numbers, object identification, spelling, and patience. Children no longer play with block sets after age three or four.

smarties.com, and www.wonderbrains.com for more information.

Farm toys

If you live in the Midwest and Plains states, "the Heartland of America," farm toys are the number one toy collectible. Collectors are primarily adults.

Manufacturer and type are the two major ways that farm toys are collected. Ertl, Racing Champions, Scale Models, and Spec-Cast are leading manufacturers. While tractors dominate farm toy collections, accessories and implements, for example, manure spreaders, are popular. Animal figures, barns, etc., allow collectors the opportunity to create an entire farm scene.

When purchasing a piece of farm equipment, it is customary to receive a miniature toy of the piece purchased. Equipment brand loyalty is paramount in farming country, and that loyalty crossed over into collecting. Collectors are loyal to the same brand equipment in their toys. A John Deere enthusiast usually does not include International Harvester toys in his collection.

In addition to purchase incentives, many companies, such as Ertl, made and/or make farm toys for sale through catalogs, department stores, and collectors' clubs. Although one can find farm toys in die-cast slush metal, plastic, and pressed steel, the vast majority are cast-iron. Farm toys are made to last, just like their full-size counterparts.

Farm toys have evolved into a separate collecting community, much like toy trains and toy soldiers. There are separate farm toy periodicals and shows. Collecting standards now match those found throughout the toy community.

Farm toys are available for virtually all modern tractor brands—AGCO (Allis Chalmers, Gleaner, Massey Ferguson, and Oliver), Case IH (International Harvester), John Deere, and Ford New-Holland. Farmall and Minneapolis-Moline also are represented by older examples.

Because farm toy collecting is centered in the farming community, its market strength and weakness also is closely related to the frequent changes in the farm economy.

Guns and military toys

The single-shot cap pistol toy arrived on the scene just prior to the Civil War. It remained a childhood favorite for over fifty years. These pistols were made by the same cast-iron manufacturers who made banks and other toys. Size, quality of design, scarcity, and working order are the collecting keys. Beware of reproductions: Period molds were discovered in the 1970s. Recasts from these molds are very hard to differentiate from period pieces.

The roll-fed cap pistol dominated the toy gun market from the late 1940s through the mid-

Ideal produced this plastic "U. S. Half Track," Model I-2748, in the early 1950s. Much of the United States military equipment used during the Korean War was carried over from World War II.

1960s. Leading manufacturers included Actoy, Classy, Esquire, Hubley, Kenton, Kilgore, Mattel, Nichols Industries, George Schmidt, Stevens, and Wyandotte. Cap guns were issued for leading movie and television cowboy heros—Gene Autry, Hopalong Cassidy, The Lone Ranger, Marshal Matt Dillon, Roy Rogers, Wyatt Earp, etc. By the late 1980s, cap pistols became an independent collecting category.

The late 1980s and early 1990s witnessed a brief collector interest in air and BB guns. It ended by the beginning of the twentieth century.

In the twenty-first century, cap guns sold in the United States have to have a bright orange, red, or

LEFT: The golden age of the toy roll-cap gun extended from the late 1940s though the early 1960s. Many of the 1950s television Westerns had licensed sets. Acquiring a set accompanied by a picture of the child who wore it is a rarity and highly prized by collectors. RIGHT: Louis Marx & Company made this lithograph tin and wood "Army Sparkling Pop Gun," Model 198, based on the semi-automatic, military model, 20 caliber rifle. Replacement sparkling metal eyelets were available.

yellow tip placed over the muzzle to avoid confusion with an actual gun.

Most military toy collectors gravitate to the toy soldier category. In the late 1980s and 1990s, there was a surge of interest in military-related toys issued during World War II.

Toy guns and military toys have all but disappeared from toy store shelves thanks to the anti-war sentiment of the 1960s and 1970s, anti-gun sentiment, and recently negative attitudes toward the war in Iraq. A brief revival in interest during Desert Storm ended within a year. Playing war is no longer fashionable among youngsters—a victim, like playing cowboys and Indians, of changing social mores.

Model kits

Until the post-1980s collecting craze, individuals purchased model kits to build them. This is no longer entirely true. Collectors now view unbuilt kits as highly desirable collectibles. Although a few collectors buy the built models, the quality can be very inconsistent.

Model airplane, car, monster, and personality kits are the most eagerly sought. There is a small,

Ambroid Models of Weymouth, Massachusetts, marketed these wood and plastic kits of World War II aircraft: S-4, F-51 Mustang; S-5, P-40 Warhawk; S-6, F4U-5 Corsair; and S-7: F6-F Hellcat. The finished models had a wingspan of 17 ½ inches.

but dedicated group of collectors who focus on military model kits. However, many individuals who buy the military related models build them. This does not hold true for collectors of other types of kits.

While type collecting dominates, some collectors focus on manufacturer, such as Aurora, AMT, Hawk, Monogram, or Revell. Scale is another collecting approach. Common scales are 1:24, 1:48, 1:72 and 1:100.

Model kits are found in a variety of skill levels. Snap-together kits are the easiest to assemble. The level of skill required is generally indicated on the box. Advanced collectors seek customized kits, those that allow the builder greater flexibility in construction.

Model kit collectors divide kits into three groups: (a) MIB, mint-in-box with period wrapping still untouched, (b) BWB, built but still retaining its period box, and (c) BNB, built but missing its period box.

This plastic model kit of the Winnie Mae was made by Lindberg Products of Skokie, Illinois. The model has forty-six parts, an instruction sheet, and a decal sheet. In 1931 Wiley Post and Harold Gatty flew the Winnie Mae around-the-world in eight days, fifteen hours, and eight minutes.

Paper dolls, soldiers, and other toys

Think beyond paper dolls and soldiers. There is more to paper toys than these two categories. Some of the earliest American toys were made by applying lithographed paper to wood. Accordion paper fold theater toys of the late Victorian era are highly prized by collectors. This category also includes die-cut, stand-up figures with painted or applied lithograph paper surfaces.

The earliest manufactured paper dolls date from the early nineteenth century. A Japanese handmade paper doll dating to A.D. 900 is known. J. Belcher of Boston published *The History and Adventures of Little Henry* in 1812, the first American paper doll book. By the 1820s boxed paper doll sets arrived on the scene.

McLoughlin Brothers and Peter G. Thompson were leading American manufacturers of paper dolls in the late nineteenth century. McLoughlin's Dottie Dimple, Lottie Love, and Jenney June were very popular. They competed with imported paper dolls from England and Germany.

Paper dolls first appeared in magazines in 1859. The craze hit its peak in the first decades of the twentieth century when magazines such as *Good Housekeeping* and *Ladies' Home Journal* featured paper doll inserts.

Samuel Lowe Publishing Company, Merrill Publishing Company, Saalfield Publishing Company, and Western Publishing Company, Whitman Publishing Company produced the paper doll books that fueled the paper doll collecting craze of the 1930s through the 1960s. Many paper doll books focused on movie star and other celebrity dolls.

ABOVE: The Whitman, #3773, *Green Acres* paper doll set contained two dolls with "stay-on" costumes. The wardrobe consisted of thirty-six pieces. *Green Acres*, Starring Eddie Albert as Oliver Douglass and Eva Gabor as Lisa, ran on CBS from September 15, 1965 to September 7, 1971. BELOW: Doll manufacturers often issued paper doll sets associated with their popular dolls to compete with the paper doll books from publishers such as Saalfield and Whitman. This Besty McCall paper doll set dates from 1953.

There is a separate advertising/paper ephemera show circuit just as there are separate doll, toy, toy train, and toy soldier show circuits. Advertising/paper ephemera shows are an excellent shopping source not only for paper toys but for boxed board games as well.

Pedal cars

Do not be confused by the name. With the exception of bicycles, the pedal car category includes any pedal toy, such as airplanes, automobiles, fire engines, tractors, and so on.

The earliest pedal cars date back to the 1890s. They closely mimicked their larger counterparts. Their cost meant their owners were primarily from wealthy families. Other children focused on ride-on toys such as the Irish Mail.

There are two golden ages for pedal cars, (a) the 1920s and early 1930s and (b) the 1950s and 1960s, the age of chain driven models. Pedal cars from the first period featured wooden chassis, sheet metal bodies, and wooden wheels with hard rubber tires. Most were generic in form. Only a few were copies of larger counterparts. Early manufacturers include American National, Garton, Gendron, Steelcraft, and Toledo.

By the mid-1950s, the pedal car was a popular gift found under the Christmas tree. Pedals cars manufactured by AMF and Murray are the most commonly found.

Pedal car collectors prefer examples in assembly line condition. As a result, examples are rebuilt and restored to the same quality standards as automobiles and other vehicles.

Pedal tractors, once part of the pedal car col-lecting community, are now a separate collecting category. The same individuals who collect and restore full-size tractors also do the same for them.

Plastic toys

The use of plastic in toy production dates to the 1930s, but it gained prominence in the post-1945 period. The first plastic toys were inexpensive generic automobile and other generic vehicle toys designed for sale in five-and-dime stores.

Following World War II, the Louis Marx Company was one of the first toy manufacturers to utilize plastic, primarily for the figures in its playsets. In the mid-1960s, concerns about lead poisoning resulted in laws banning toys made of lead, thus opening the door further to the use of plastic.

American plastic toy manufacturers competed with Japanese manufacturers in the late 1950s and early 1960s. By the mid-1960s and early 1970s, the majority of plastic toy manufacturing was centered in Hong Kong. By the 1980s, the manufacturing of plastic toys shifted to China, which today dominates production in this category.

Several "plastic" toys have their own collecting category, for example, action figures, Barbie, and G.I. Joe. Collecting divides with toy categories such as Fisher Price and Tonka Trucks are marked by the replacement of an older primary material such as wood or press steel by plastic.

Premiums — radio, cereal, television, and fast food

Premiums are promotional giveaways that either come with a product or are acquired by sending in proof of purchase, sometimes in addition to a small payment. When collecting, do not neglect the advertising, offer sheets, and product boxes on which the offer appeared.

The mid-1930s through the mid-1950s was the golden age of radio premiums. Although most were sponsor-related, some simply promoted a show. Almost every popular show, ranging from Jack Armstrong (1933–1951) to The Lone Ranger (1933–1955) to Fibber McGee and Molly (1935–1957), offered premiums of some type.

The late 1940s through the 1960s was the golden age of cereal premiums. Wheaties, the Breakfast of Champions, issued a series of airline stickers, coin sets, a Hike-O-Meter, sports card sets, and a host of other premiums in the 1950s. Millions of boxes of National Biscuit Company's Nabisco shredded wheat were eaten to obtain Injun-Unity cards. Kellogg's was especially active issuing sets of pinback buttons featuring cartoon characters and World War II military insignia and planes. Many of its early 1940s box backs featured plane cutouts.

A 1999 Pizza Hut K'NEXosaurus & Friends fast food, construction toy premium. The series consisted of four different bags of parts used to build a variety of objects. Not all fast food toy premiums are movie and television licensed.

Just as with radio, television show sponsors offered a wide variety of premiums. Nabisco was a sponsor of the *Rin-Tin-Tin* television show. Premiums included a bugle call vinyl cardboard record, cast photo, and a variety of rings. By the 1980s, the majority of television premiums were Saturday morning cartoon related.

McDonald's is king of the hill in the area of fast-food collectibles. As the competition for customers intensified, fast food chains began issuing licensing premiums.

Most premium collectors focus on one media or show. There are form collectors, the largest group being those who collect premium rings.

Premium collectors were one of the principal groups responsible for the 1970s/1980s collectibles revolution, the period when collecting mid-to-late-twentieth century toys as opposed to late nineteenth century and pre-1945 toys became acceptable.

A 2001 Kellogg's Spider-Man water squirter in its period packaging. Although the mid-1940s through the mid-1960s was the golden age of cereal premiums, cereal manufacturers still use them.

Pressed-steel toys

Collectors divide pressed-steel toys into three chronological periods: (1) pre-1920; (2) 1920 through 1962; and (3) 1962 to the present. It is the second of these periods that collectors consider the golden age of pressed-steel toys.

Most collectors focus on manufacturer. Buddy L is king of the hill, even in the twenty-first century. Other leading manufacturers include Tonka, Smith-Miller, Structo, and Wolverine. American collectors prefer American-made examples, and collecting crazes focusing on makers occur.

Construction equipment and trucks are the two forms most sought after by collectors. Some collectors have built specialty collections by focusing on airplanes, buses, farm equipment, emergency vehicles (the name commonly used for post-1960 firehouse toys), racers, and ships.

As the generation who grew up with them ages, interest is increasing in pressed-steel toys from the 1960s and 1970s. Tonka is the king of the hill in this later period. Until the past few years, pre-1962 examples, the period when rubber rather than

The Moline Pressed Steel Company, Moline, Illinois, began making pressed-steel "Buddy L" vehicles in 1921. Plastic wheels replaced rubber wheels in the early 1960s. By the late 1960s, vehicles also were made from plastic.

plastic was used for wheels, held the most collector interest. Emphasis is now changing to examples made between 1963 and the end of the 1970s.

Pressed-steel toy collectors, like their pedal car counterparts, tend to restore their finds to factory new condition as opposed to leaving them in "played with" condition. Trade literature is filled with advertisements from manufacturers who supply replacement parts and decals.

Puzzles

Puzzles divide into two basic groups: (1) jigsaw, i.e., puzzles that assemble into pictures and (2) mechanical, i.e., those that require dexterity or mental manipulation to solve. American and English collectors focus primarily on jigsaw puzzles. European collectors love mechanical puzzles.

Jigsaw puzzles divide into four distinct periods: (1) eighteenth and nineteenth century puzzles; (2) puzzles made between 1905 and 1920; (3) puzzles made between 1920 and 1940; and (4) post-1940 puzzles. Most jigsaw puzzle collectors want puzzles designed for adult or family use. Collectors place a premium on wood-cut puzzles over die-cut card-

Hasbro produced this reissue of the 1949 Tonka 1:18 scale Dump Truck in 1999 as part of Tonka's fiftieth anniversary celebration. Like many modern toys, it was made in China. Most collectors never removed it from its box.

Doing puzzles was a popular pastime during World War II. Companies such as Jaymar and Tuco sold puzzles featuring military and patriotic home front scenes.

board puzzles. Most children's puzzles are bought by crossover collectors—for instance, a Hopalong Cassidy collector might acquire a Hopalong Cassidy frame tray puzzle.

Milton Bradley, McLoughlin Brother, Parker Brothers were the three leading jigsaw puzzle manufacturers at the beginning of the twentieth century. Milton Bradley and Parker Brothers lead the 1930s transition from the adult wood to the family cardboard puzzle. Tuco (The Upson Company, Lockport, New York) was a leading manufacturer of cardboard puzzles from the mid-1930s through the 1950s. Springbok Editions, acquired by Hallmark in 1967, launched in 1964. Wrebbit's "Puzz-3D" puzzles first appeared in 1991.

There are dozens of ways to collect puzzles. Some collectors seek puzzles with specific surface images, such as artwork by identified illustrators or World War II patriotic images. Others collect a specific maker, such as Parker Brothers, or a type, such as advertising, Depression era craze (1932-1933), mystery, or television-licensed.

Collectors' Club: Association of Game & Puzzle Collectors (197M Boston Post Road, West Marlborough, MA 01752; www.agpc.org)

Robots and space toys

In an effort to revive the Japanese economy following World War II, U.S. toy importers like Cragstan, Marx, Mego, and Rosco contracted with Japanese toy manufacturers such as Daiya, Horikawa, Masudaya, Nomura, Yonezawa and Yoshiya to produce friction or clockwork, stamped steel toys. The first post-war robot toys appeared on the market in the late 1940s.

There were early American-made robot toys. Ideal's Robert the Robot appeared in the *1954 Sears Christmas Book*. Marx's Electric Robot, Marvelous Mike, and Z-Man followed. However, when Japanese manufacturers introduced battery-operated robot and space toys, they quickly and completely dominated the American market.

The first robot collecting craze occurred in the mid-1970s, driven in large part by American collectors of battery-operated toys. Japanese buyers

The original incarnation of *Battlestar Galactica*, starring Lorne Greene as Commander Adama, aired on ABC from September 17, 1978 to August 4, 1979. Although short-lived, the show had a number of licensed products including this 1978 Parker Brothers boxed board game.

Cragstan's Mr. Atomic is considered by many collectors the most desirable of the post-1945, battery-operated robot toys. The toy had three different actions. A reproduction, easily confused with the period toy by a novice, was reissued in the late 1990s.

and space toy collectors fueled another craze during the late 1980s and early 1990s.

Collectors seek lithograph tin robots and space toys, largely ignoring plastic examples. As in other categories, the period box is critical.

In theory, this category also includes comic-, movie-, and television-related space toys, such as Buck Rogers and Flash Gordon from the comics, *Battlestar Galactica*, *Space 1999*, *Star Trek*, *Tom Corbett Space Cadet*, and more from television, and *Alien* and *Star Wars* from the movies. In truth, many of these subcategories are major collecting categories in their own right.

Tin toys

This category comprises lithographed tin toys manufactured from the late nineteenth century through the present. Collectors divide the category chronologically: (a) late nineteenth century through 1920; (b) 1920 to 1942; (c) 1946 to 1980; and (d) post-1980.

German toy manufacturers, such as Lehmann, dominated the first of these periods. When supply was cut off during World War I, it opened the door for American manufacturers to enter the market. Collectors view the 1920 to 1942 period as the Golden Age of lithograph tin toys, an era when Chein, Girard, Marx, Ohio Art, Unique Art, and Wolverine held sway. Japanese manufacturers of inexpensive lithograph tin were active competitors to the American firms. In the decade immediately following the end of World War II, Japanese manufacturers along with a few German manufacturers such as Schuco drove American manufacturers from the market.

Collecting by manufacturer or toy type are the two main collecting focuses. Chein and Marx are the American favorites. 1950s and 1960s Japanese-

William Britain, Sr., developed a method to hollow-cast toy soldiers in 1893. William Britain, Ltd., quickly replaced German manufacturers as the leading maker of cast toy soldiers. Collectors place a premium on sets still in their period boxes.

The 1920s through the 1950s, with the exceptions of the period from 1941 to 1945, were the golden age of Marx lithograph tin toys. Marx introduced Jazzbo Jim in the early 1920s. The base and box are marked "Jazzbo Jim The Dancer on the Roof."

made vehicles, especially those modeled after actual vehicles, were hot in the 1980s and early 1990s.

Many lithograph tin toys produced after 1946 are collected by crossover collectors from other toy categories. Robots and vehicles are two examples.

Collectors' Club: Ohio Art Collectors Club (18203 Kristi Road, West; Liberty, MO 64068; www.geocities.com/ohioartcollectors/)

Toy soldiers

Collecting toy soldiers is one of the oldest forms of toy collecting, dating back to the Renaissance. This is a male, adult-driven category. Although designed initially for young boys, toy soldiers—like miniature dollhouse furniture—quickly evolved into an adult toy. Toy soldiers are often displayed in large-size battlefield dioramas.

Most collectors focus on maker, with Britain being king of the hill. Actually hundreds of companies made toy soldiers. Prior to 1945, toy soldiers were made of lead or composition, a mixture of sawdust and glue. Plastic soldiers were intro-

duced in the late 1940s. Inexpensive bagged sets of twenty or more unpainted soldiers sold for less than one dollar in the 1950s. Even Britain switched to plastic in the mid-1960s, a move followed quickly by Cherilea, Crescent, and Timpo. In the mid-1970s, a cottage industry devoted to the resurrection of the hand-painted lead soldier occurred. Collectors eagerly seek figures from companies such as Blenheim, Marlborough, Nostalgia, and Tradition.

Toy soldiers are classified as (1) mass-produced, (2) handcrafted, and (3) blanks painted by skilled or amateur painters. Kits for the home casting of toy soldiers were popular from the 1920s through the 1950s in the United States, and this practice is still strong in Europe.

Soldiers were sold as single figures and in sets. This is a collecting category where set value is a premium and the period box or packaging is essential.

Toy soldier can both mean military figure and civilian figure. But civilian figures, unless they portray an actual person, are rarely as sought after as their military counterparts.

Toy trains

The earliest toy trains did not run on tracks. They were pull or floor toys made of cast-iron or tin. The electric toy train achieved popularity at the dawn of the twentieth century. From the beginning, toy trains played a major role in Christmas platforms. It was not until after World War I that the toy train layout was left up and running all year long.

The mid-1920s through the late 1950s was the golden age of toy trains. American Flyer, Ives,

A. C. Gilbert American Flyer rolling stock from the late 1940s—650-R Passenger Coach, 636 Wire Car, and 635 Wrecker Car. Trains could be purchased as sets or as individual units.

Lionel, and Marx produced electric model trains that featured highly detailed casting and markings. A slow conversion to plastic occurred within the industry in the late 1950s and early 1960s. Trains are collected first by company and second by gauge. Lionel is king of the hill, followed by American Flyer. As a result, O, O27, and S are the three most popular gauges among collectors. Collector interest in HO gauge trains is increasing, but interest in N gauge is minimal.

There have been several major shifts in collecting emphasis over the past decade. First, post-World War II trains have replaced pre-war trains as collector favorites. Second, new companies, such as MTH (Mike's Train House), introduced engines with modern electronic sound technology and other special features and offered reproductions of many hard-to-find engines and rolling stock. Third, platform accessories, from buildings such as houses and train stations to landscape items such as tunnels, are enjoying a renaissance.

Specialized toy train shows remain extremely popular. They, more than any other type of specialized toy show, attract family groupings, that is to say, grandfather, father, and son attending the show together.

Collectors' Clubs: American Flyer Collectors Club (PO Box 13269, Pittsburgh, PA 15243); Ives Train Society (21 Academy Street, Forestville, NY 14062); LBG Model Railroad Club (68 Haienda Circle, Plantsville, CT 06479); Lionel Collectors Club of America (PO Box 479; La Salle, Illinois 61301; www.lionelcollectors.org); Marklin Enthusiasts of America (PO Box 21753, Charlotte, NC 28221); Marklin Club—North America (PO Box 510559, New Berlin, WI 53151; www.marklin.com); Toy Train Collectors Society (109 Howedale Drive, Rochester, NY 14616); Train Collectors Association (PO Box 248, Strasburg, PA 17579; www.traincollectors.org)

Vehicles

Along with toy soldiers, toy vehicle collecting has the oldest collecting history within the toy community. Every material category—cast-iron, diecast, pressed-steel, and wood—includes vehicles.

Vehicles are collected primarily by type: airplane, automobile, fire equipment, horse-drawn, motorcycle, racer, trolley, and truck. Collectors can

ABOVE: Although the Drowst Manufacturing Company had been making cast toy vehicles since the beginning of the twentieth century, it first used Tootsietoy in 1921 and trademarked it a few years later. Tootsie was the name of Theodore (Ted) Dowst's daughter. The Airflow Chrysler dates from 1935–36 and the Buick from 1927. BELOW: Kenton made this cast-iron "Seeing New York/Sight Seeing Auto," circa 1905 to 1910. Examples in the Lillian Gottschalk and Jack Herbert collections are well known to advanced collectors. The Sailor sits at the wheel. Behind him are Happy Hooligan with his spinach can hat; Happy's brother, Gloomy Gus; the Professor; and Mama Katzenjammer with her familiar red hair top knot.

focus on manufacturer time period, and material in each subcategory.

Realism is critical. Collectors prefer detailed miniature examples of their full-size counterparts. They want to be able to identify the vehicle by manufacturer and year. There is some flexibility in respect to paint scheme. Most collectors shy away from generic examples.

Vehicle collectors have a checklist mentality, a necessity in a collecting category where variants prevail. Checklists are available through reference books and collectors' clubs.

The category is global. Collectors often seek both foreign-made and American-manufactured examples.

Vehicle collector clubs are generally based on manufacturer. Hot Wheel and Matchbox are the two best examples. Multiple clubs and websites exist in support of both.

Collectors' Club: Toy Car Collectors Association (PO Box 1824, Bend, OR 97701)

Windup toys

European manufactured spring-driven windup toys entered the American toy market at the end of the nineteenth century. They were inexpensive and provided strong competition to the more expensive American-made clockwork toys.

American manufacturers responded. Sehlesinger was the leading American producer of windups prior to 1900. Examples of Sehlesinger windup toys are extremely difficult to find and coveted by collectors.

As the new century dawned, other American toy manufacturers entered the market—Julius Chein

J. L. Hess, Nuremberg, Germany, manufactured this lithograph tin touring car with a clockwork friction mechanism around 1910. The figure is composition.

(1903), Strauss (1914), and Louis Marx (1920s). E. R. Ives & Company introduced a windup train. Marx quickly gained market dominance thanks to his colorful lithograph tin bodies and marketing acumen.

The popularity of spring-driven toys waned following World War II. Chinese and Japanese manufacturers are responsible for almost all post-1945 windup toys sold in America. Collector interest in the latter is minimal.

Collectors tend to focus on specific chronological periods or on a single manufacturer, such as Lehmann, Marx, or Strauss. Surface imagery and amount of surviving paint are important value considerations.

America experienced several yo-yo crazes, one in the late 1920s to early 1930s and another in the late 1940s and 1950s. Cherrio challenged Duncan's market supremacy in the latter period. The back of the box has instructions in English, Spanish, and French. "Yo-yo" is absent from the text on the box, instruction sheet, and yo-yos in order to avoid legal action by Donald Duncan.

Collectors prefer windup toys in working order since hidden mechanism is often difficult to remove for repair without causing serious damage to the toy. Further, replacement mechanisms are not easily acquired.

Wooden toys

Wooden toys date back to antiquity. Construction sets, blocks, and carved figures (action and static) are just a few examples. This category includes toys made from wood with applied paint decoration as well as wooden toys with applied lithographed paper designs. There are two main categories of wooden toys, mass-produced and handcrafted.

Wooden toys made during World War II have evolved into a separate collecting category. Many materials such as iron, plastic, steel, and rubber that were used for toy production were required for the war effort. Wooden guns, model kits, toy soldiers, and vehicles became the order of the day.

Wooden toys are collected by type, for example, the yo-yo. Fisher-Price collectors divide their collecting category into toys made fully from wood, albeit hand-painted and often with applied lithograph paper, and those constructed from a combination wood and other materials such as plastic.

Wooden toy collectors largely ignore home-made 1920s and 1930s Depression-era toys and basement workshop toys from the 1920s through the 1960s.

Identifying the Toys You Are Going to Collect

Take time to explore what kinds of toys are available on the market by visiting museums, attending toy shows, talking with collectors, and reading the available literature. Once you have made your decision on what to collect, you are not bound to stick with it. If you find that other toys are catching your interest you can always change your focus and start over again. You may choose to expand your collecting interests or even have several different collections at the same time.

General Considerations

You need to accept the fact that there are factors that will place limits on what and how you collect. Available funds, space, and time are the three most important.

Collect what you can afford. "Afford" means being able to buy a high-end example two to three times a year. Why frustrate yourself by collecting a toy category in which you can only afford lesser quality items?

Toys are no fun if you do not have adequate space to display and play with them. If your space is limited, create a specialized collection that contains between fifty and two hundred pieces. Be aware that collections have a bad habit of filling the space allotted to them.

Thanks to the Internet, time no longer is as critical as it once was in building a collection. The Internet allows you to hunt globally in a relative short period of time. Remember, the Internet is no substitute for getting out in the field and interacting with others. Collecting is as much about people as it is about the objects.

The Toy King

Alfred Carlton Gilbert (1884–1961) was an athlete (he won a gold medal in the pole vault at the 1908 summer Olympics in London), businessman, inventor, and toymaker. Born in Salem, Oregon, he died in Boston, Massachusetts.

The A. C. Gilbert Company of New Haven, Connecticut, introduced over half a dozen toy classics. These include chemistry and other scientific sets, erector sets, and magic sets. In 1938 Gilbert took over the American Flyer Corporation, making it one of the premier toy train companies of the post-1945 period.

In 1916 A. C. Gilbert was one of the founders and first president of the Toy Manufacturers of America (TMA). In 1941, Gilbert created the Gilbert Hall of Science in New York City, one of the country's first science and technology museums.

Gilbert retired in 1953 and turned his company over to his son. The family divested itself of its holdings following Gilbert's death in 1961, and A.C. Gilbert went out of business six years later.

ABOVE: Better to spend your money on one quality item rather than three or four less quality items is a good toy collecting rule. Patience and a willingness to hunt eventually will allow you to find a quality item as this 12″ Shirley Temple doll and gift set, circa 1959. BELOW: Storage kits for action figures often feature great graphics. They also are very affordable. This *The Real Ghostbusters* action figure case is copyright 1988 and based on the characters from the Saturday morning cartoon, not the movie.

Points to remember

Here are some tips to remember no matter what toy category you decide to collect.

Tip #1: The toys you are collecting were mass-produced. You do not have to buy the first one you see. Insist that any toy you buy meets your collecting standards.

Tip #2: The quantity of toys made is far greater than you realize. Milton Bradley produced over 400,000 Hopalong Cassidy games. U.S. Time made over six million Hopalong Cassidy watches. This was in the 1950s. Imagine what the production numbers must be today. Assume there are more examples of any toy in attics, basements, closets, garages, and sheds than in the marketplace.

Tip #3: The survival rate for toys is higher than you realize. Do not buy into the "one of the only examples known" mindset.

Tip #4: Keep in mind Rinker's Thirty Year Rule: "For the first thirty years of anything's life, all its value is speculative." This rule was developed in the mid-1980s to explain the constantly fluctuating values of contemporary collectibles.

You cannot create instant long-term collectibles. Cabbage Patch dolls, Tickle Me Elmo, Holiday Barbie, and Beanie Babies proved this point over and over again. All speculative bubbles, even for older toys, eventually burst.

Why thirty years? It takes thirty years for the generation that played with a group of toys to reach maturity, become nostalgic, and decide to recapture their childhood. Thirty years is the minimum required for objects to achieve a stable secondary resale market value, assuming, that they have interest to the collecting community.

Many objects will simply be forgotten and vanish.

Tip #5: Supply may exceed demand for all toys made after 1980. America became collecting conscious around 1980. The general public realized the old toys they threw out had collector value, so they started storing them rather than discarding them. This ensured a higher survival rate than normal.

Collectors also realized that it made sense to buy new toys in their collecting category when they first appeared rather than waiting for them to enter the secondary market and paying a premium. However, instead of buying one toy, they often bought multiples and starting hoarding them.

The general public jumped on the bandwagon. If a new toy was in short supply, demand increased and prices far in excess of retail were paid. Most speculators will never recover the money they spent.

Tip #6: There are a limited number of collectors for every toy. Often that number is one hundred or less. Once all these collectors have acquired an example of a specific toy, the remaining examples have little to no value. It is possible to saturate the market. Scarcity fluctuates. You need to constantly track the market.

Globalization of collecting

Today's collecting marketplace is global. This is especially true for toys. America's toy tradition is European-based. In the nineteenth and early-twentieth centuries, American toy manufacturers largely copied European toys. America did not start producing its own jigsaw puzzles until the 1850s. Prior to that and for nearly a hundred years afterward, puzzles were imported from England and Europe.

Europe has a strong toy collecting tradition. Admittedly, the focus is on eighteenth, nineteenth, and very early-twentieth century toys, while American collectors dominate the post-1945 toy scene. When visiting Europe, keep your eyes open for doll, toy, and toy train museums. You will find all three in Nuremberg.

American and European collectors compete actively for toys, and the arrival of the Internet only

Kenner issued this Scorpion Alien action figure in 1992. Its long-term collectibility remains to be determined. It has over ten years to go before it falls outside Rinker's Thirty Year Rule.

Hoarding was prevalent among collectors by the time this Hess Toy Truck Bank was issued in 1987. When offered for sale on eBay, the final price rarely exceeds its initial cost.

intensified this competition. Prior to 1980, American collectors won most of the competitive values simply by being willing to pay more. Today the playing field is far more level.

In addition, collectors from Japan and elsewhere have discovered the fun of collecting toys. Although initially concentrating on buying toys produced or marketed in their homelands, foreign collectors have greatly expanded their collecting focus. American television Western toys enjoy a strong market in Japan and well as Germany.

After 1945, American movies, music, and television influenced the world. American culture and the products associated with it were marketed worldwide. As foreign collectors discover the fun and funk of post-1945 toys, they are turning their attention to the American market. In the late 1990s and first few years of the twentieth century, Japanese collectors were the primary buyers for Raggedy Ann and Andy dolls and anything Peanuts related. Recently, they have shifted their attention to Strawberry Shortcake. Today one has

to think globally to understand the secondary market value of toys.

Finally, the Internet has created a new division in toys—in fact in the world of collecting as a whole—

German collectors love the American West and classic American television cowboy shows. *Bonanza*, dubbed in German of course, was extremely popular in Germany. German collectors compete actively on eBay and other American Internet sites for *Bonanza* material.

Matchbox licensed its toy vehicles worldwide. In order for a collection to be considered representative, it must include foreign-licensed examples. This Matchbox set was licensed for sale in Japan.

those that have local appeal versus those that have global appeal. The former consists of toys that can only be sold in their country of origin, such as 1930s Sun Rubber toys. They hold little-to-no interest to foreign collectors. The latter comprises toys that can be sold worldwide. Barbie, Disneyana, and Matchbox are three examples. The first clue to identifying this group of toys is to look at how they were marketed. If the toy was marketed worldwide, chances are it has a worldwide collecting base.

Worldwide marketing is not the sole criteria. An advanced American collector of tin toy vehicles has no trouble adding an example made in France but never sold in the United States to his collection. However, these examples tend to reflect the high end of the market. There is little-to-no interest in the common examples.

Thinking in broad, general terms is the key to understanding toy collecting. Time and experience allows you to refine your thinking process.

This Kingsbury Golden Arrow racer is the epitome of great streamlined Modernist design. It is as much an art object as a toy.

5 **10** 2

5

THROWING
THE BULL

ⅬＤＲ
IN U.S.A.

DIRECTIONS

This Game subject is taken from
the popular western sport of
"THROWING THE BULL."

To play, stand the Bull in the
base and stand about 8 feet away.
The first player tosses the rings
and counts his score as follows:

The Ring on the tail counts 5, one
horn 5, the other horn 10, and over
the entire head 25. The other
players then follow in rotation.
The player first totaling 100,
throws the Bull and WINS, provided none of the other players
total a higher score in the same
number of throws.

CHAPTER THREE

SIX ADDITIONAL APPROACHES TO COLLECTING TOYS

Chapter Two introduced thirty major collecting categories, although the number of sub-categories is vast. Dolls, teddy bears, and plush toys were grouped together, but in actuality each is a separate, stand-alone collecting category. The same holds true for mechanical and still banks.

The toy collecting categories in Chapter Two divide into two distinct sub-groups—by form and by material. Form describes the function of an object. Action figures, banks, dolls, jigsaw puzzles, toy trains, etc., are forms. Forms are found in an endless variety of shapes, materials, and surface decoration. Most toy forms subdivide into two or more major subcategories.

Many collectors, especially those aged fifty and above, collect by material. Eight of the thirty collecting categories from Chapter Two are focused on material. While this approach is declining among younger collectors, it currently remains one of the main approaches to toy collecting.

Your imagination is the only restriction on how toys are collected, but there are a few standard approaches to collecting toys that enjoy great favor with toy collectors. This chapter explores six of them.

OPPOSITE: Throwing the Bull game.

Collect by Manufacturer

Children and adults are brand loyal. An American Flyer toy collector would not own Lionel rolling stock. Toy collectors often fall in love with the products of a single toy manufacturer. When they do, they establish the goal of acquiring an example of every toy the manufacturer produced. Aided by extensive research in reference books, copies of sale catalogs, and information obtained from other collectors, they prepare a checklist that is used as a collecting guide.

Older toy collectors know Marx primarily as a manufacturer of lithograph tin toys, such as the 1931 Little Orphan Annie Skipping Rope. Younger toy collectors, those who grew up between the mid-1960s and 1970s, know Marx as the manufacturer of playsets featuring metal carrying cases and buildings and plastic figures and accessories.

This approach to toy collecting can require a lifetime commitment, and it is quite likely that the goal of a collection comprising every example known may be impossible. What can be accomplished is assembling the most complete collection known to collectors.

Many toy manufacturers make a wide variety of toy forms from a number of different materials, such as Louis Marx and Company who made toys ranging from lithographed tin toys to plastic playsets. As a result, toy collectors often concentrate on a specific toy type from a single manufacturer. Mattel marketed a great many dolls but most Mattel doll collectors focus on Barbie.

The Geographic Approach

Although toys were made by hundreds of manufacturers scattered across the country, there were pockets of toy production. Review the locations of toy manufacturers provided in Chapter One. The Connecticut River Valley and eastern Pennsylvania between Philadelphia and the Lehigh Valley are two locations that housed dozens of toy manufacturers. Rubber toys came from the rubber-belt towns of northeastern Ohio, such as Auburn and Barberton. Ask a toy collector to name the location where farm toys were made. Over 90 percent will answer Dyersville, Iowa, which at one point was the home to Ertl and several other manufacturers.

Local toy collectors tend to collect locally made toys. A Shimer cast-iron, horse-drawn toy made in Shimerville, Pennsylvania, is highly prized by eastern Pennsylvania collectors. Cast-iron toy collectors living elsewhere may not hold it in the same regard.

In today's highly mobile world of overseas manufacturing, local and regional loyalty, especially in the collecting sphere, is rapidly diminishing. Most local and regional toy collectors are well beyond sixty years of age. Many are donating their collections to historical societies and museums.

There is a small but dedicated number of toy collectors who collect toys made in one country—America, Canada, England, France, Germany, Japan, etc. In most cases, these collections are further limited chronologically. Just because you are from a particular country doesn't mean you have to collect it; a number of American toy collectors specialize in collecting German-made toys.

Collect by Theme

A third popular way to collect toys is by a particular theme. The possibilities are endless. Foreign costume dolls, comic characters, television cowboy hero toys, and space toys are just four examples. Do not confuse form and theme collecting. They are very different. A form is the basic toy. Theme is shape and pattern (decoration).

Collecting by theme does not have to be limited to toys alone; they may only be part of the collection. This is especially true when the theme is a fictional character, celebrity, movie, or television series. Although a Roy Rogers bedspread is not a toy, no toy collector would be surprised to find it for sale at a toy show or in a toy auction. A *Planet of the Apes* collector has no problem exhibiting a costume from the show next to a licensed toy.

Theme collectors divide into two primary groups. The first consists of collectors who strive to have one example of every known toy in their

ABOVE: The majority of "Big Bang" collectors are located in Eastern Pennsylvania. Bethlehem, Pennsylvania, was home to the Gas Cannon Company which became the Toy Cannon Works in 1916 and The Conestoga Company, Inc., in 1924. The company is best known for its Big Bang Cannon, although it also made an airplane and tank. The "bang" comes from firing bangsite, a calcium carbide mixture. BELOW: Dolls made in Germany are a favorite focus of traditionalist doll collectors. This 1920s, 15-inch high, German doll has a bisque shoulder head, cloth lady's body, bisque hands, mohair wig, and painted eyes. The maker is unknown.

Toys are only one segment in character and personality licensing. This Roy Rogers jigsaw puzzle was a cereal premium. Is a Roy Rogers and Dale Evans lunch kit a toy? The answer is no, but it would most certainly be found in a Dale Evans and Roy Rogers collection.

collection. Their approach mirrors that of the "manufacturer" collection. The difference rests in the fact that the theme collector often is dealing with dozens of different toy manufacturers, making his or her collecting task much more demanding.

A collection focusing solely on pre-1940 newspaper comic characters would number in the hundreds of objects. Richard Outcault's *Yellow Kid* is one of the earliest comic characters; his daily comic strip started in 1896.

Adaptation is the Key to Survival

In 1894 John E. Hubley and a group of investors founded Hubley Manufacturing Company in Lancaster, Pennsylvania. The company initially manufactured electric toy trains.

In 1909 a fire destroyed the Hubley plant. The company relocated to the factory of the defunct Safety Buggy Company. The move and destruction of its molds took a financial toll on the company; eventually, Joseph T. Breneman and John H. Hartman headed a new group of investors who purchased the company.

A large toy order from Butler Brothers, a leading wholesale jobber, saved the company. However, instead of toy trains, Butler Brothers wanted cast-iron hardware, novelties, and toys. Hubley switched to making horse-drawn vehicles, toy guns, and a host of other cast-iron toys.

Hubley survived the Depression by introducing a line of automobiles, motorcycles, trucks, and other vehicles. It focused on toys retailing for a nickel, dime, or quarter.

Following World War II, Hubley began branding with national companies. Its Bell Telephone truck was one of the most popular toys of the 1950s. Hubley also switched from cast-iron to die-cast metal to create its toys. After being purchased by Gabriel Industries in 1965, Hubley made toys from plastic as well as die-cast metal.

By adapting, Hubley remained a leading American toy manufacturer for close to 100 years.

Collectors who are satisfied with a sampling of toys in their collection comprise the second group, and they often buy the common and inexpensive toys. The toys are a part of but often not the centerpieces of their theme collections.

Type Collection

Variety is the spice of life in a type collection. A type collection focuses on depth and breadth by comparing and contrasting similar toys from different manufacturers, locations, etc.

A collection of a particular type of die-cast vehicle from every manufacturer in the world who made that vehicle is one example of a type collection. Another is a collection consisting of examples of every toy form manufactured by Louis Marx and Company. A third is a collection of wooden toys made throughout the world.

Toy collections focusing on fixed chronological periods are type collections. The length of a chronological period can be as short as five years—such as World War II toys—or as long as half a century—such as early-nineteenth-century dolls. Most chronological collections span a ten- to twenty-year period or focus on time periods that reflect changes in lifestyle or a specific generation. Toy collectors break the post-1945 period into three distinct time units: (1) 1946 to 1962; (2) 1963 to 1979; and (3) 1980 to the present. Toys can also be divided from the era of black-and-white television, color television, and the computer age.

Collect by Age, Gender, and Family

Toys can play a major role in shaping who we become as individuals, how we interact with

Vehicle collectors tend to focus on automobiles. However, specialty collectors have assembled large collections of airplanes, motorcycles, trucks, and ships. Fleischmann, a German manufacturer known primarily for its HO scale trains, made this painted tin ship in the 1920s.

others, and how we define our place in society. Parents throughout time have viewed toys as a way to teach sharing and group interaction skills. Today's parents focus on the educational and developmental value of toys.

How about the role toys play in stereotyping, especially in what is male and what is female? Hasbro has a Boys Toys division. Would you be surprised to learn that it does not have a Girls Toys division? The vast majority of toys are designed for boys, and video games are a great example.

ABOVE: The cover image on Renwal Blueprint Models The Visible V8 kit clearly indicates it is a boy's toy. The kit is copyrighted 1960, has over 100 moving parts, and comes with a "How An Auto Engine Works" manual. RIGHT: The box graphics on the 1950s Junior Miss Sewing Kit says it all. This is a girl's toy. The instructions tell girls how "to make dolly dresses." BELOW: The Home Shopping Club's "Limited Edition" Vanna doll, available in twelve different outfits, is clearly a toy designed to appeal to girls and women.

When children are little they tend to be given gender-based playthings. Girls receive dolls and housekeeping toys while boys receive action figures and vehicles. Given the advances in the feminist movement in the 1970s and 1980s, you might have thought things would have changed, but largely these trends still continue today.

When examining the thirty collecting categories in Chapter Two, consider who is more likely to collect a particular toy, a boy or a girl? If you make a checklist, boys win hands down.

Action figures and vehicles are the two largest boys' toys collecting categories. Until the 1980s, toy trains were a close third. Dolls, dollhouses, teddy bears, and stuffed toys are girls' toys. If a boy receives a teddy bear, he is likely to discard it at an early age.

Many women are avid doll, teddy bear, and stuffed toy collectors. However, domestic training toys, such as kitchen sets and toy appliances, do not garner much collecting interest. Children's dish sets are an exception.

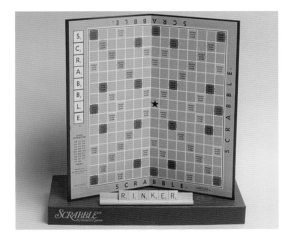

ABOVE: Alfred Moshe Butts of Poughkeepsie, New York, invented Scrabble. Originally called Lexiko and then Criss Cross Words, the game was first sold in 1948. When Macy's placed an order for Scrabble in the early 1950s, its success was ensured. Over a hundred million games have been sold. LEFT: Kitchen toys perpetuate the role of women as happy homemakers. Many toys, such as the Micro Mix mixer, mimic the actual appliances found in mommy's kitchen. BELOW: Boxed board games such as this 1950s Howdy Doody game were billed as fun for both boys and girls.

Parents, not children, collect infant—also known as pre-school—toys. They are the individuals who remember purchasing these items and watching their children enjoy them. Toy memories for children begin at age six or seven, and very few remember their infant toys. Rattles, playpen toys, walkers, and block sets may be among the first toys children receive, but they are often discarded as soon as the children outgrow them. Next come a host of pull and musical toys, again quickly discarded.

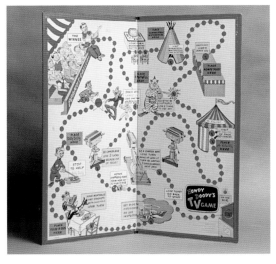

Hasbro returned G.I. Joe to his 1964, full 12 inch size in the early 1990s in hopes of reviving the franchise. In 1992 Hasbro issued a special collection edition Hall of Fame series consisting of Ace, Destro, Gung-Ho, and Storm Shadow.

Collect by a Single Toy

Some individual toys have reached the point where they are their own specialized collecting category. Barbie, G.I. Joe, and Matchbox are the three most obvious, but there are many others.

When non-collectors look at a single toy, they often fail to see the variants that exist. Toy collectors become acutely aware of them. A complete Marx playset collection would contain over one hundred examples. Many individual playsets were made in six or more variations.

There is a large variety of toys that are designed for family play. Boxed board games, tabletop games, and some jigsaw puzzles are examples. Most of these toys are generic as they were produced over an extended period of time in fairly large quantities.

Manufacturers have long recognized that adults buy toys. There are dolls, dollhouses, toy trains, and toy soldiers manufactured primarily for sale to adults. In the late 1980s toy manufacturers found a market in "Collector Edition" toys—high-priced, never meant for play, and directed exclusively at the adult market.

Barbie and Ken found themselves outfitted as characters in movie epics such as *Gone With the Wind* and television shows such as *Star Trek*.

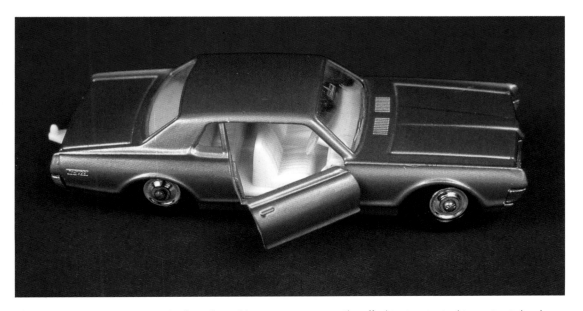

This Mercury Cougar K-21 was the first of Matchbox's KingSize cars. The off-white interior in this version is harder to find than the ones that were issued with red interiors.

Tracking down variants and even knowing they exist can be challenging for the collector. A reference book focusing only on Matchbox variants has recently been published—color is the principal variant in vehicles. A reissue with a new set of accessories is common in the action-figure category.

Beware of artificially created variants, that is, variants that were not produced by the manufacturer. This problem is endemic in the toy soldier collecting category. Do not accept anyone's word without independent corroboration from a second source.

Unique prototype toys—internal design models of toys produced for study by the manufacturer—are among the most highly prized toys in this collecting approach. Models of toys which were ultimately not produced are more highly prized than the models for the toys that were. Since prototypes are among the few one-of-a-kind collectibles within toy collecting, they sell from the high hundreds to the middle thousands of dollars.

In Conclusion

Toy collectors often mix approaches within a single collection. They select the display methodology that is right for them. Display methodology is only one of the many aspects of toy collecting that allows individual self-expression. Just as no two collectors are identical, no two toy collections will ever be the same.

CHAPTER FOUR

TOOLS OF THE TRADE

Although a toy is an inanimate object, it can come alive through your research as you ask and uncover the answers to questions such as who made it, how was it made, how was it marketed, how was it played with, who played with it, why was it saved, how does it relate to other playthings of the same era, and finally, what is its value and how is its value determined? Building and studying your own personal reference library is essential to having a well-researched collection and gathering an accurate picture of a toy's history.

Building a Reference Library

Reference books are a necessary expenditure so that you can properly research and identify your toys. Many collectors are loath to invest in costly specialized reference books, especially when it seems like information is readily available on the Internet. Avoid developing an "I'd rather spend money on toys than reference books" mentality. You need to be well-informed before making a purchase. In order to achieve this, you need a good reference library.

How much money should you expect to spend per year to acquire reference material? If you are just getting started, consider allocating between $300 and $500 on assembling a core library.

OPPOSITE: The proper tools are crucial when painting intricate models and toy soldiers.

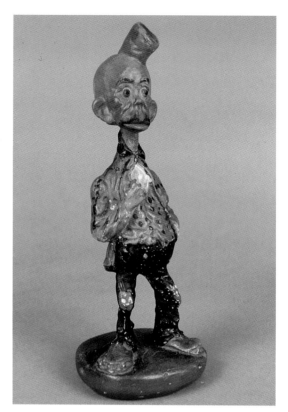

Can you identify this early comic strip character? If you cannot, why would you collect it? His name is Happy Hooligan, a creation of Frederick Opper. Now that you know this, do some research and find out more about him.

own home as opposed to doing research at a library or in the home of another collector.

The One Book to Own if You Are Only Going to Own One

Which is more valuable—knowing where to find information or knowing what something is worth? Experienced collectors do not need price guides. Their field experience is their guide. Even beginning collectors rapidly develop an intuitive sense of secondary market value.

The one book you need to own, the one book that you cannot do without, is David J. Maloney Jr.'s *Maloney's Antiques & Collectibles Resource Directory*, published by Krause Publications. Make certain you buy the most current edition. It is likely to be the first book you grab off the shelf when beginning a research project.

Known in the trade simply as *Maloney's*, the book provides information about appraisers, auction sources, buyers, collectors, collectors' clubs, dealers, experts, museums, periodicals, restoration

Then, budgeting between $200 and $300 a year should allow you to maintain your library.

It is likely that as your collecting sophistication grows and you begin to seek the harder-to-find secondary paper ephemera items, such as advertising displays and other material and/or manufacturers' catalogs, you may need to double your research library budget.

Never question for one minute that this is not money well spent. It can be tremendously satisfying to research a toy within the confines of your

Want to know more about this *Welcome Back Kotter* boxed board game? *Maloney's* is an ideal source to put you in touch with collectors, dealers, experts, and collectors clubs relating to television memorabilia and boxed board games.

supplies and services, and a wealth of other information for more than 3,000 collecting categories. There are more than 20,000 listings, of which more than 11,000 have website information and 14,000 have e-mail addresses.

Publishers You Need to Know About

Although there are dozens of publishers who have published one or two specialized toy reference sources, there are six publishers with extensive lists:

Collector Books (PO Box 3009, Paducah, KY 42002; www.collectorbooks.com)

House of Collectibles, an imprint of Random House (1745 Broadway, 13th Floor, New York, NY 10091; www.randomhouse.com/house of collectibles)

Kalmbach Publishing (20127 Crossroads Circle, Waukesha, WI 53187; www.kalmbach.com). Toy train titles, e.g., Greenberg Pocket Price Guides

Krause Publications, a.k.a. KP Books (700 East State Street, Iola, WI 54990; www.krause books.com)

Schiffer Publishing, Ltd. (4880 Lower Valley Road, Atglen, PA 19310; www.schifferbooks.com)

You can write or e-mail each of these publishers and ask to be put on their catalog mailing list. Examining their websites can be informative as well.

Additionally, all toy periodicals contain book reviews and often advertisements from the publishers. The reviews can be the best way to learn of toy reference books from other publishers.

The Power of Observation

Charles Pajeau, a tombstone cutter from Evanston, Illinois, introduced the prototype for Tinkertoys at the 1915 New York Toy Fair. Stuck in a corner, Pajeau failed to make a single sale. Down but not out, Pajeau talked to the owners of two drugstores in New York's Grand Central Terminal and convinced them to stock his toy. Pajeau created a window display of buildings and structures that could be made from Tinkertoys to help promote his toy. He even hired men to sit in the windows and build Tinkertoys structures. The public loved the toy.

What inspired Pajeau to create Tinkertoys? The idea came from watching children play with empty wooden spools of thread and knitting needles. Pajeau developed the concept by adding more holes to increase the play possibilities. It took him two years to perfect his toy.

Collector Books, House of Collectibles, and KP (Krause Publications) have all published specialized *Star Wars* price guides. Most titles have been revised several times and are used as checklists by serious collectors.

ABOVE: A collection of general price guides for dolls. Do not just buy one. Buy them all and compare prices. Also check the prices found in these guides against prices realized on eBay and other Internet selling sites. BELOW: A collection of general price guides for toys. The coverage differs from guide to guide. Recent editions of O'Brien's *Toys & Prices* focus heavily on select post-1945 toy categories. Make certain the guide covers the toys in which you are interested before buying it.

General Price Guides

While you may only need one general toy price guide, I recommend investigating them all. The key is to find the general toy price guide that works best for you and then buy each edition of that guide as it is published. Do not discard your old general toy price guides. They are important research tools.

Check out the following:

Foulke, Jan. *Jan Foulke's Guide to Dolls*. Bangzoom Publishers.

Hake, Ted. *The Official Hake's Price Guide to Character Toys*. Gemstone/House of Collectibles.

Herlocher, Dawn. *200 Years of Dolls*. Krause Publications.

Huxford, Bob and Sharon. *Schroeder's Collectible Toys: Antique to Modern Price Guide*. Collector Books.

O'Brien, Karen. *Toys & Prices*. Krause Publications.

Test the prices in these guides against those you find in the field and on eBay to determine which are the most accurate.

Specific Price Guides

There is a price guide for every specialized collecting category. In many cases there are half a dozen or more titles.

Start your reference library by buying those titles which are still in print. Many specialized price guides remain in print for only a short time, often no more than a year or two. It is a rare title that is revised and reissued in a new edition.

A good specific guide contains three basic pieces

of information: a well-researched history of the toy including a detailed history of the manufacturer(s) and manufacturing method, a checklist (often pictured) of the toys in the collecting category, and values. The history and checklist remain valid long after the values are no longer relevant. This is why out-of-print toy references often command premium prices on the secondary market.

Specialized price guides range from the general, such as a price guide to farm toys, to the highly specific, such as a price guide to Matchbox variants. Remember that a specific toy often crosses over into a multitude of collecting categories; information about a Hopalong Cassidy game may be found in a price guide devoted to boxed board games, to cowboy heroes, to television memorabilia, or to Western collectibles. As a result, a good toy reference library has a wide range of titles.

Some toy categories will have many different guides devoted to them. It is always a prudent idea to confirm and verify information by utilizing a number of independent sources.

Support Literature

The best reference libraries have a large collection of support literature, i.e., paper ephemera relating to the collector's toy interest. The most commonly found ephemera are manufacturers' catalogs, manufactures' sales literature, mail-order and other mailing pieces that include toys, store advertising, and booklets and sheets that came packaged with toys. Support literature also includes runs of collectors' club bulletins and newsletters and reproduction catalogs.

Is there a specific price guide for your favorite toy category? Chances are there is more than one. Toy shows often contain one or more bookseller who specialize in toy titles. These specialty booksellers also advertise in *Antique Toy World*.

Many collectors also seek publications that include a story about their favorite toy or have a story in which the image of their favorite toy appears. What you may think is a rare occurrence actually happens quite frequently. Once you start to look for this material, you will be surprised at how many examples you will find.

Classic Titles and Finding Out-of-Print Books

It is likely that the majority of books that belong in your toy reference library are out of print. Many such books are considered classics, such as:

Freeman, Ruth and Larry. *Cavalcade of Toys.* Century House, 1942.

The catalogs of toy manufacturers are an excellent research tool to determine when toys were first introduced into the marketplace. Today, many catalogs are online and not issued in print format.

Hertz, Louis H. *The Toy Collector*. Funk & Wagnalls, 1969.

O'Brien, Richard. *The Story of American Toys*. Abbeville Press, 1990.

Pressland, David. *The Art of the Tin Toy*. New Cavendish Books, 1976.

Whitton, Blair. *Toys*. Alfred A. Knopf, 1984.

Williams, Anne D. *Jigsaw Puzzles: An Illustrated History and Price Guide*. Wallace-Homestead, 1990.

There are dozens more. When you learn of an out-of-print title, check it out at your local library. If you only need a few pages, you can photocopy the information you need in the book at a far cheaper price than acquiring the title.

Two good websites to locate out-of-print titles are www.abebooks.com and www.bookfinder.com. Since you are not buying the book for investment purposes, condition does not matter as long as all the information is there. A surprising number of out-of-print reference books appear for sale on eBay. Always check this source first. It may take several months to find a title, but persistence and patience count.

When a toy collection is sold at auction, the reference library and support literature is often sold as well. Watch display and classified auction ads for box lots of antiques and collectibles reference books. The auctioneer almost always groups the titles by subject matter. Most reference books sold at auction are sold at bargain prices.

Toy Periodicals

There are three basic groups of toy periodicals: (1) general periodicals, a combination of magazines and newspapers that cover broad collecting categories such as dolls, toy trains, toy soldiers, and toys; (2) periodicals devoted to one specific toy collecting category such as action figures; and (3) collectors' club newsletters. Most periodicals are published monthly, although a few are issued quarterly.

Collectors should subscribe to general periodicals and specialized periodicals in their area of interest. Join collectors' clubs, even those that only deal peripherally with your primary collecting focus. Collectors' club periodicals often feature research information not available in books or on the Internet. General periodicals can be purchased at most chain bookstores. Do not discard past issues. A "run" of several years of any one of these periodicals becomes a major reference source.

Dolls

Antique Doll Collector (PO Box 239, Northport, NY 11768; www.antiquedollcollector.com) focuses on antique and vintage dolls, doll clothing and accessories, doll houses and period rooms, and antique and vintage Teddy Bears. The magazine's emphasis is pre-1940. Issues contain articles by doll experts, reports on auctions and shows, a calendar of events, and advertising from a cadre of worldwide antique doll dealers. Extensive coverage of the meeting of the United Federation of Doll Clubs is an annual feature.

Dolls (Jones Publishing, Inc., PO Box 5000, Iola, WI 54945; www.dollsmagazine.com) deals occasionally with antique and vintage dolls, but its principal emphasis is on contemporary dolls. Competition for its annual awards is fierce. Service listings include information on doll clubs and doll hospitals.

Doll Reader (Ashton International Media, 44 Front Street, Worcester, MA 01608; www.dollreader.com) provides the broadest coverage—antique, vintage, and modern—of all the doll magazines. It even covers paper dolls. As with *Dolls*, it is weighted more toward post-1945 dolls with strong coverage of the contemporary doll market.

Toys

Antique Toy World and *Toy Shop* dominate the toys, games, and puzzles periodical field. Each serves a separate community. Consider subscribing to both, even if your collecting interest applies to only one.

Antique Toy World (PO Box 34509, Chicago, IL 60634) covers the middle and high end of the market. Each issue contains three to four articles dealing with the history of toys plus reports on toy auctions, shows, and collectors' activities. Its advertising is its greatest strength. Finally, *Antique Toy World* tracks the world scene, reporting on foreign shows and containing advertisements from the leading foreign dealers.

Toy Shop (700 East State Street, Iola, WI 54990; www.toyshopmag.com) focuses primarily on toys made after 1945, although it covers some auctions of older toys. Each issue contains up to a dozen separate articles. A multiple-page price guide devoted to a major subcategory, for instance Western toys, is a regular feature. Finally,

Collectors are likely to find additional information about this Arranbee 14″ Nanette walker doll in *Antique Doll Collector* and/or *Doll Reader*.

Toy Shop also reports on new toy releases of interest to collectors.

Toy trains

Kalmach Publishing of Waukesha, Wisconsin, dominates the toy train periodical marketplace. In addition to *Classic Toy Trains*, Kalmbach also publishes *Model Railroader Magazine* and *Trains*. Toy trains are one of the few collecting categories where the hobbyist still plays a role. Scratch builders work side by side with collectors of mass-produced pieces.

Classic Toy Trains (Kalmbach Publishing Co., 20127 Crossroads Circle, Waukesha, WI 53187; www.kalmbach.com) focuses primarily on contemporary toy trains produced by firms such as K-Line, Lionel, and MTH (Mike's Train House). An occasional article will deal with obsolete rolling stock.

Toy soldiers

Old Toy Soldier (PO Box 13324, Pittsburgh, PA 15243; www.oldtoysoldier.com) has been published since 1976, changing ownership in 2001. Company histories and identification articles are a specialty. Coverage includes civilian as well as military figures.

Specialized Periodicals

Dozens of toy sub-collecting categories have their own periodicals. *Lee's Toy Review* (PO Box 322, Monroe, CT 06468; www.leestoyreview.com) and *Toy Farmer* (Toy Farmer Publications, 7496 106th Avenue, La Mourne, ND 58458; www.toyfarmer.com) are just two examples. *Maloney's Antiques and Collectibles Resource Directory* is an

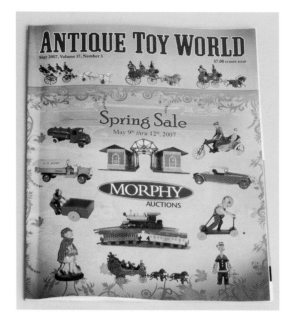

Dale Kelley's *Antique Toy World* magazine is the bible for traditional toy collectors. When presented with a chance to buy back issues, do it. Serious collectors keep a complete run of twenty-plus years on their shelf.

excellent source to determine if there is a specialized periodical that covers your particular area of collecting interest. The reference librarian at your local public library also can help you locate this type of information.

Collectors' Clubs

Many toy subcollecting categories have their own collectors' clubs. Chapter Two contains collectors' club information for many of the categories discussed and *Maloney's* can provide information on any category that isn't mentioned.

In addition to joining the collectors' club(s) covering your specific toy interest, also consider joining the broader clubs such as:

Antique Toy Collectors of America, c/o Susan Het-
tinger, 764 Twilight Drive, Crescent Springs,
KY 41017

Association of Game and Puzzle Collectors, 197M
Boston Post Road, West, Marlborough, MA
01752; www.agpc.org

National Model Railroader Association, 4121
Cromwell Road, Chattanooga, TN 37421;
www.nmra.org

Toy Soldier Collectors of America, PO Box 179,
New Ellentown, SC 29809; www.toysoldiers
collectors.homestead.com/tsca.html

United Federation of Doll Clubs, 10920 North
Ambassador Drive, Suite 130, Kansas City,
MO 64153; www.ufdc.org

Past Giants

Many toy periodicals lasted for only a few years.
Yet during that time, many well-researched articles appeared in print. Occasionally runs of these
periodicals appear for sale on eBay or at auction.
When given the opportunity, consider purchasing
them.

Here are some titles to watch out for:

Collectibles Illustrated
Toy Collector Magazine
Collectibles Monthly
Toy Shoppe (the newspaper)
Collectors Corner
Toy Values Monthly

If you purchase a boxed board or card game such as Bunco, and it does not have the rules, do not fret. The Association of Game and Puzzle Collectors maintains a file of rules and is happy to provide them for you if available.

Websites

Information on the Internet can be minutely precise or shamefully ignorant. Because anyone can post any information they want, not everything that is posted is truthful. Question all information you see on the Internet. Because so much information is copied between websites and blogs, you may find yourself confirming false information with identical false information. Compare Internet information with that found in printed sources.

If something does not make sense or you find conflicting information, ask an advanced collector for his opinion. Remember, you are asking for his opinion which, once again, may not be correct.

The simple truth is that more information about toys, especially production records, is unknown than known. Guesstimates are common. There is really no substitute for doing your own research using period sources.

Supplies

Collecting toys does not require a great number of supplies. With the exception of a digital camera, loupe, magnet, and black light, most supplies are used to display or store toys. It's worth taking the time and effort to find the appropriate supplies. Spend the funds necessary to buy quality and uniform supplies, and learn how to use the supplies correctly.

Inspection/buying equipment

Most toys are good sized. You can see what you need to see with your eyes. A triple reflex ten power loupe may be useful to spot the smaller details and can be purchased from any jewelry supply house. It uses three pieces of magnifying glass, the result of which is that the surface is in focus across the entire lens. (Simple magnifying glasses are only in focus in the middle.)

You can also take a trip to your local stationery store and buy a reading glass. While the magnification may be lower, the surface is much bigger, big enough to see anything you need to see when inspecting a toy.

A horseshoe magnet helps identify cast iron and pressed steel if the toys you collect have these materials. A digital camera is an excellent way to make a record of an object for further study. Buy a camera that takes excellent, in-focus close-up images.

Another tool that some collectors use is an ultraviolet light, used to detect repaint and some repairs. When the surface of a toy exhibits an uneven color surface, some repair or restoration has occurred. However, a skilled collector can use his hands and eyes to detect repairs and restorations, often catching many the ultraviolet light does not reveal. Collectors who use ultraviolet lights may be tempted to rely on them too heavily.

Display cases and storage supplies

Antique Toy World and *Toy Shop* contain advertisements for individuals selling display cases and storage supplies. Most large toy shows have several dealers selling supplies. Doll auctioneers such as Harris McMaster sell display cases and other supply needs of the doll collector. Many collectors purchase cardboard storage boxes, use plastic containers, and tubs available anywhere.

Most supplies are not archival quality and many cardboard and plastic containers are not acid free or inert. Ninety-nine percent of the time, there is no problem. However, when your collection reaches the point where it is home to several high-end pieces, think about investing in archival quality supplies for display and storage of your most valuable items. You can purchase archival quality supplies at your local art store, by placing an order in conjunction with an order being placed by your local historical society, library, or museum, or through Internet sites.

Proper supplies and display cases do not guarantee the safety of your toys. If you misuse the supplies, such as putting a display case on a windowsill exposed to sunlight, damage will occur. If you ever need to move your collection, take special care to purchase the proper packing supplies and wrap them carefully to ensure that your items arrive in one piece.

Restoration and repair supplies

Restoration and repair supplies are available at your favorite art store or Internet supply sites. If your item is valuable, consider hiring a trained professional to do the repair or restoration.

Most toy collectors own a magnifying glass or 10X loupe for the purpose of accurately reading marks and checking for hidden damage and restoration.

CHAPTER FIVE

FINDING TOYS

Finding toys to add to your collection can be an exciting challenge for the collector. Toys can be found in many locations, such as flea markets, church sales, tag sales, antiques malls, estate auctions, and on the Internet. One important factor for the savvy collector is finding a toy that is complete and in fine or better condition.

Your first toy buys are likely to be those items you remember from your childhood—the toys you had as well as those you wish you had. When you find them, you may experience a strong nostalgic feeling. Take care not to let these feelings cloud your judgment.

Establish your own set of buying criteria and stick to them. Keep your criteria simple, such as "I will not buy the toy unless it is complete, in the condition I desire, priced at what I am willing to pay, and I have money in my pocket to buy it." Apply your criteria to every item you consider buying and be willing to walk away if the toy doesn't measure up.

The hunt is part of the collecting mystique, and part of the joy of toy collecting is that there are numerous hunting ranges for toys. Sharing information is an important part of collecting. Knowing where to buy well is one of the most valuable pieces of information in the antiques and collectibles trade.

OPPOSITE: View-Master.

Start in Your Own Basement or Attic

What happened to your childhood toys? If you are lucky enough to find them, chances are they will be in disarray. As a child you played with them and you had no concerns about their long-term collectibility. When you were done playing, you threw them, not always carefully, into the toy box.

Once you discover the location of your toys, whether attic, basement, closet, garage, or shed, your first task is to put the toys back together again. Your goal is to create complete toys, locating and matching all the parts to the correct toys. Chances are high that the parts will be scattered or missing entirely. Replacement pieces can be purchased on the Internet or at an antiques toy show.

Keep an eye open for boxes and packaging, as these items are often stored in a separate area. In

LEFT: The film, *Beetlejuice,* was released in 1988, followed by the production of a line of *Beetlejuice* dolls and collectibles by Kenner. Many collectors bought large quantities when the toys were eventually sold at discount. ABOVE: This hand painted, cast-iron elephant still bank has been in my bedroom since I was an infant. I am now in my mid sixties. My toy collection began with the toys I saved from childhood.

fact, they may have been recycled and used for storing non-toy items. Do not assume they are lost until you confirm this.

You can also ask other family members and friends if they have any old toys packed away in a basement or attic that they would be willing to give you.

Garage Sales/Church Bazaars

Buying toys at garage sales requires patience. The tendency is to grab and pay for a toy the moment you see it. It is important that you do not let your emotions get the best of you and that you take time to thoroughly examine the potential purchase and apply your buying criteria.

Start examining the toy by focusing on whether or not it is complete. If parts appear to be missing, look around as they may be present, just misplaced. Do not hesitate to ask the seller if he or she knows where the missing parts are located.

Tip: Never take the seller's word that a toy is complete. The responsibility to determine this rests with you.

The best toy buys are found in older neighborhoods. Toys sold at garage sales in new developments where younger families prevail generally only have recycle or reuse value. To find older toys you must seek out the sales in neighborhoods dominated by older individuals, those ready to retire or already retired.

You need to be a proactive buyer when shopping the garage sale circuit. It never hurts to ask if you do not find the toys you are seeking. The seller may own them but never have given much thought that someone might be interested in buying them.

Always make certain electronic games work before buying them. If found at a garage sale, ask to use an electrical outlet and plug in the game. Also look for accompanying parts. Make your offer to buy once you have found all the pieces available.

Create and carry business cards that state I BUY TOYS and provide your name, a telephone number, and an e-mail address. Do not include your home address for security reasons. If you specialize, change I BUY TOYS to I BUY 1950s TV WESTERN TOYS or whatever your special interest is, and distribute these cards generously.

Since you cannot go to every sale, consider running a string of garage sale pickers to look for toys that may be of interest. These are the garage sale regulars who are out every weekend. Ask them if they would be willing to act as your buying agents. They can contact you when they find something so you can authorize the buy. Pickers normally expect to double the purchase price and be paid in cash within twenty-four hours.

If you only have limited time to devote to garage-sale shopping, keep an eye open for neighborhood and community garage sales where multiple families will have items for sale in the same location.

Church bazaars and white elephant sales can be great toy hunting grounds. In many cases, the donors are older individuals and many toy bargains can be found at these events.

Newspaper Advertisements

Many collectors get their best buys through newspaper advertising. The cost to advertise that you buy toys in the classified advertising section of your daily newspaper can be expensive. The local penny press—the shopping newspapers you find at grocery stores and restaurants—is the place to spend your advertising dollars.

A classified advertisement needs to run for three to six months in order to be effective. This is why the inexpensive advertising rates of the penny press have appeal.

When advertising, stress that you are a private collector. Individuals prefer selling to a private collector rather than a dealer. Their assumption, and perhaps rightly so, is that a private collector will pay more.

Many antiques and collectibles trade papers have one or more pages devoted to "business card" advertising. While modest, the cost can add up. In reality, "business card" advertisements are more for the specialized advanced collector than for the novice collector.

Flea Markets

There are many types of flea markets, ranging from antiques and collectibles flea markets where older toys are likely to be sold to swap meets where discontinued and modern toys are found. Once a great buying source for toys, these venues have fallen on hard times in the twenty-first century thanks to the growth of specialized toy shows and the Internet.

Today's flea market sellers are professionals, moving on a daily basis from flea market to flea market. The age when locals cleaning out a basement or garage rented a table to sell is long past. Professional flea market sellers are price savvy, often asking near-market prices for what they have to sell.

Also, there are more reproductions (exact copies), copycats (stylistic copies), and fantasy items (toys that did not exist historically) for sale at flea markets than at any other venue. If you find a toy at a bargain price at a flea market, examine it carefully to make absolutely certain you know what you are buying.

Most flea markets are held outdoors; as a result, toys offered for sale are often

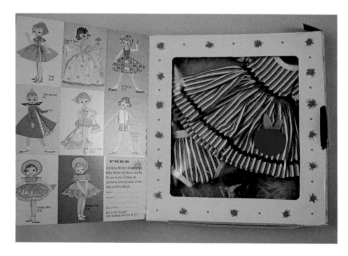

Placing an inexpensive classified advertisement in a penny saver that reads—"Want to buy Betsy McCall outfits in their boxes. Call ____," is an excellent way to add to your collection.

There are thousands of toys that are not listed in price guides, including skateboards. Just because they are not listed does not mean there are no collectors for these toys, such as this Roller Derby Deluxe #20 skateboard.

dusty or dirty. Dust and dirt can easily hide defects, so take extra time to examine any toy you encounter.

If you decide to hunt in the flea market jungle, consider going when an antiques and collectibles oriented flea market stages an "extravaganza" or special event weekend. A flea market tends to double or triple in size during an extravaganza weekend. The weekend also attracts piggyback shows, special events at nearby antiques malls, and local garage sales.

There are dozens of flea markets, some seasonal, monthly, or weekly, that have extravaganza weeks. Some follow a regular pattern. Others vary the dates. Here are a few favorites as well as some monthly markets:

- Adamstown, Pennsylvania: Black Angus, Renninger's, and Shupp's Grove
- Alameda, California: Alameda Point Antiques and Collectibles Fair (first Sunday of every month)
- Atlanta, Georgia: Scott Antiques Market (second weekend of every month)

- Brimfield, Massachusetts: (second weekend in May, July, and September)
- Canton, Texas: First Monday Trade Days (Friday before the first Monday of each month)
- Charlotte, North Carolina: Charlotte Antique and Collectible Show, formerly Metrolina (first full weekend in April and November)
- Kutztown, Pennsylvania: Renninger's (last full weekend of April, June, and September)
- Long Beach, California: Long Beach Outdoor Antiques and Collectibles Market (third Sunday of each month)
- Mount Dora, Florida: Renninger's Twin Markets (third weekend in January, February, and November)
- Springfield, Ohio: Springfield Antiques Show and Flea Market (third weekend of the month of May, July, and September)
- Portland, Oregon: Portland Expo (March, July, and October)
- St. Charles, Illinois: Kane County Flea Market

Antiques Malls

The antiques mall arrived on the scene in the early 1980s, and it reached maturity in the late 1990s. Antiques malls grew from small malls featuring thirty to fifty dealers to supermalls housing hundreds of dealers. Adamstown, Pennsylvania, is home to an "Antiques and Collectibles" Mile—more than a dozen antiques malls open seven days a week, similar to an Auto Mile where a dozen or more car dealerships are located in a strip.

Beginning in the late 1990s, antiques malls began to specialize. A mall focusing primarily on

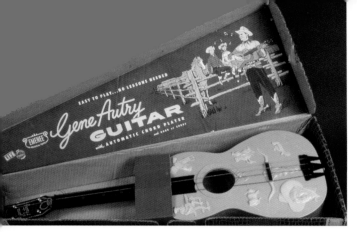

Toy dealers are reluctant to expose expensive merchandise to the sun, dirt, and other hazards associated with outdoor flea markets. This Gene Autry guitar in its period box is most likely to be found for sale at an antiques mall or antiques toy show.

decorating accessories or exclusively serving the decorating trade is the most common. However, there are specialized toy malls. Big Kill Collectible Toy Mall & Retro Store (14109 Burbank Boulevard, Sherman Oaks, CA) and the South Louisville Antiques & Toy Mall (4150-8 East Bluelick Road, Louisville, KY) are two examples.

Bargains are few and far between. Most antiques mall sellers are experienced professionals. They have extensive research libraries and are very familiar with top market toy prices. Some toy sellers use antiques malls to house their inventory between shows.

Most toys offered for sale at an antiques mall are in very good or better condition. Antiques mall toy sellers stock toys that appeal to advanced, not novice collectors.

Malls are great places to do comparison shopping. If you find a toy that catches your fancy, make a note and check out what the identical toy brings on eBay and in Internet storefronts.

Do not fall victim to the "if I do not buy it when I see it, it will be gone when I get back" mentality. Toys, especially when close-to-market price, sell slowly at antiques malls. You may lose a toy or two along the way, but you will save money in the long run by not purchasing hastily.

The Internet

The Internet is more than eBay. The Internet includes four basic selling sources: (1) storefront sites such as go www.antiques.com, www.ruby lane.com, and www.tias.com: (2) individual seller websites; (3) eBay: and (4) auction bid venues like www.liveauction.com and www.proxibid.com, in which you can bid using the Internet during a live auction.

Many of the middle- and high-end toy sellers maintain stores within storefront sites, which are individually owned and operated store within a larger Internet site. Like the toys found at antiques malls, toys offered in these stores tend to be higher grade, very good and better, and priced toward the

The Internet, especially eBay, is playing an increasing role in toy sales to collectors. It also is helpful in researching a toy. Since there is little editing or fact checking of information posted on the Internet, use a second or third source to verify what you find.

high side. The sellers are hoping to attract the advanced collector.

A few toy dealers have their own Internet sales sites. Check out www.antiquetoy.net, www.toy drummer.com and www.zipstoys.com. You can add to the list by culling website addresses from several issues of *Antique Toy World*.

eBay is the major buying venue for common and middle range toys. eBay is so powerful that the values realized are an accurate reflection of what the toy is worth. Using eBay, huge collections can be built at bargain prices for the buyer with patience and persistence.

One admonition, be careful not to catch "auction fever," a disease that compels you to be the last bidder standing no matter what the price. If you cannot control your competitive bidding instincts, use a sniping service such as www.esnipe.com.

The Internet is still in its infancy. Look for more and more toy-buying opportunities in the years ahead. However, the Internet will never fully replace face-to-face buying. There will always be individuals who demand to personally inspect and handle a toy before they buy it.

Auctions

Lloyd Ralston Toys pioneered the specialized toy auction. By the mid-1980s more than a dozen other individuals jumped aboard the bandwagon. Even Christie's and Sotheby's entered the fray. Finally, several toy brokers teamed up with auctioneers to offer auctions devoted exclusively to toys.

Toy auctions divide into two basic types—catalog and non-catalog. While advanced collectors concentrate on cataloged sales, novice collectors

A Few Quick Tips for Using eBay

1. eBay.com is just the tip of the iceberg. It is eBay's American site. Check out www.eBay.ca (Canada), www.eBay.co.au (Australia), and www.eBay.co.uk (United Kingdom), eBay's other English language sites. If you can read German, visit www.ebay.de. eBay's homepage contains a full list of all the countries in which eBay has a separate website. Thanks to PayPal, paying for toys bought abroad is relatively trouble-free.
2. Use the "question" feature to query the seller about any concerns you may have before bidding.
3. Do not necessarily plan to buy the first example you see. Check completed auctions to determine the price point you are willing to pay. Often the fifth or sixth example offered on eBay garners considerably less than the first two examples.
4. Factor shipping costs into the price you bid. In some cases, you may pay more to have the item shipped to you than you paid to buy it. If an item is particularly large, heavy, or delicate and the seller is nearby you may wish to make arrangements to pick it up directly.
5. Check payment options before bidding. Some sellers only accept a specific type of payment such as money orders or PayPal.

should check out their local auction houses to see how they handle toy sales.

Almost every estate auction includes toys. If the number is too small for a specialized sale, they are sold with the general merchandise. It is good practice to scan the local auction advertisements. Then if you see toys listed, attend the preview and check out the toys. Never buy at this type of auction without personally inspecting the toys.

Auction catalogs are an excellent source to track the high-end of the market. Collectors make a point to obtain a list of prices realized and then file the catalogs in their reference library.

Do not be surprised if you encounter spirited bidding on the better toys. Auction pickers—individuals representing advanced collectors and dealers—are regular attendees. Auctioneers know who they are and often alert them in advance. The good news is pickers have a value limit. If you are willing to exceed it, chances are strong you will finish as the successful bidder.

Strong regional auction houses, such as Sanford Alderfer Auction Company (501 Fairgrounds Road, Hatfield, Pennsylvania), occasionally offer specialized non-cataloged doll and toy auctions. In some cases, they may utilize an Internet bidding site for a portion of the lots.

Catalog toy sales focus on the middle and high ends of the market. Most major toy collections are sold via this venue. Ten years ago, most catalogs were available in print format. Today, most specialized auctioneers post their catalogs on the Internet.

The growth of the Internet has increased competition at these auctions, as bidding now occurs on a global basis. Even if the toys sold are beyond your means, you should make a practice of reviewing the catalogs and prices realized. In fact, printed catalogs with prices realized are one of the major reference sources used by advanced collectors to check market value.

There are four types of specialized toy auctions—dolls, toys, toy soldiers, and trains. The following is a sample of some of the leading auctioneers.

Dolls

McMasters Harris Auction Co. (PO Box 1755, Cambridge, Ohio; mcmastersharris.com)

Theriault's (PO 151, Annapolis, MD 21404; theriaults.com)

Toys

Noel Barrett (PO Box 300; Carversville, PA 18913; www.noelbarrett.com)

Bertoia Auctions (2141 De Marco Drive, Vineland, NJ 08360; www.bertoiaauctions.com)

Hake's Americana and Collectibles (1966 Greenspring Drive, Timonium, MD 21093; www.hakes.com)

Every major American toy auction is advertised in *Antique Toy World*. *Antique Toy World* also runs follow-up auction stories highlighting the pieces sold, identifying some of the buyers, and discussing trends.

LEFT: This Gebruder Heubach, 10-inch high, bisque socket head, mold #8192, composition Flapper body doll is typical of the type of dolls found in doll auctions and at doll shows. RIGHT: Dolls often appear in series, such as this Alexander 11" Lissy McGuffey Ann, #1258, from the "Dolls from the Classics" series. Collector interest often varies considerably for each doll of a series.

Randy Inman Auctions, Inc. (PO Box 726, Waterville, ME 04903; www.inmanauctions.com)

Morphy Auctions (2000 N. Reading Road, Denver, PA 17517; www.morphyauctions.com)

Richard Opfer (1919 Greenspring Drive, Timonium, MD 21093; www.opferauction.com)

Lloyd Ralston Toys (549 Howe Avenue, Shelton, CT 06484; www.lloydralstontoys.com)

Toy soldiers

Joseph F. Saine Toy Soldiers (628 Dixie Highway, Rosford, Ohio 43460; www.josephsaine.com)

Trains

Bertoia Auctions

Ted Mauer (1003 Brookwood Drive, Pottstown, PA 19464; www.mauerail.com)

Lloyd Ralston Toys

Stout Auctions (529 SR 28 East, Williamsport, IN 47993; www.stoutauctions.com)

Trading or Swapping

Trading among collectors is not as common in the twenty-first century as it was in the twentieth. The lack of fixed rules makes most collectors uncomfortable, and achieving a win-win situation can be difficult. Developing an apple-to-apple comparison is the key to fair trading. A great deal of trading takes place without the mention of value, but this does not make sense since value is a constant measure. If the two individuals involved in the trade can agree on the value of each object in the trade, the playing field is leveled.

If you think trading will work for you, give it a try. You will know after the first or second experience if this is a satisfying approach to building your collection.

Is Baywatch Barbie worth the same amount as Dr. Barbie? While Barbie price guides suggest the answer is yes, two collectors considering a trade rely on their own perceived value, in which case the answer may be no.

Toy Show Circuit

The specialized antiques and collectibles show exclusively devoted to toys arrived on the scene in the 1970s. As a collector, you have three goals when attending a toy show: (1) buy, (2) make dealer contacts, and (3) meet and talk with other collectors. Toy shows should add to your knowledge as well as your collection.

Most toy show sellers also sell directly to the buyer, on the Internet, and at antiques malls. When you find a dealer who is offering the type of toys you like, make his or her acquaintance. Get the dealer's business card and give him or her a list of your wants and needs. In today's low-inventory, quick-sale environment, you want the dealer to contact you when he or she finds a toy you want.

There is no way you can attend all the toy shows, so it is more effective to pick a few favorites and attend them regularly. When dealers identify you as a regular show attendee, they will put items aside and bring them to the show specifically for you to see first.

Much of the selling at a toy show takes place two or three days in advance of the show. Dealers tend to favor one or more local hotels or motels. In the days prior to the show's start they often sell out of their rooms. Just roam up and down the

Dolls quickly work their way into the doll auction and show circuit. Character and personality dolls, especially those related to comic, movie, music, and television licenses, are the only dolls that might be found at an antiques toy show.

Unlike dolls, game and puzzles collectors do not have their own separate show circuit. Puzzles and boxed board games, such as this *Bionic Woman* game, are found at antique toys shows.

halls and corridors and stop in those rooms that have toys of interest.

The toy show circuit is sophisticated. Dolls, toy trains, and toy soldiers have their own separate show circuits. Locate them through the trade periodicals specifically designed for these collectors. Also check out www.dollshow.com and www.greatrainexpo.com.

There are hundreds of local and regional toy shows as well as large antiques shows that have a strong toy component. Here is a sampling:

- Allentown Toy Show, Allentown, Pennsylvania Fairgrounds
- Atlantique City, Atlantic City, New Jersey Convention Center; www.atlantiquecity.com
- Arizona Toy Round-up, State Fairgrounds
- Chicago Antiques & Collectible Toy and Doll World Show, Kane County Fairgrounds; www.chicagotoyshow.com
- Das Awkscht Fescht Toy Show, Eyer Jr. High School, Macungie, Pennsylvania
- Dan Morphy's Antique Toy, Doll, Holiday and Advertising Show, York, Pennsylvania Fairgrounds; www.aagal.com

- Kalamazoo, Michigan Circus Maximus Antique Toy and Pedal Car Show, Kalamazoo Fairgrounds
- Miami Antique Toy Show, Intercontinental West Miami Hotel
- Northland Antique Toy, Doll, and Advertising Show, Progress Center, Minnesota State Fairgrounds
- Rochester Antique Toy Show, Minnet Hall at Monroe County Fairgrounds; www.oldtoysonline.com
- Toronto Toy, Train, and Doll Collectors Show, International Centre, Mississauga, Ontario, Canada; www.antiquetoy.ca

In Conclusion

Finding toys requires time and a dedicated commitment to tracking sources. Collecting is never work when you devote yourself to having fun and making it an adventure by allowing yourself to get caught up in the excitement of the hunt. Try not to forget the joy of collecting and challenge yourself to keep this foremost in your mind.

CHAPTER SIX

WHAT'S IT WORTH?

There are no fixed values for antique and collectible toys. A toy's value is dependent upon circumstances, place, and time. A toy is worth only what someone is willing to pay for it. Also, in the twenty-first century, the secondary market for any antique and collectible toy is subject to the collecting whims and trends of the moment.

Grading Toys

The first step to determining the value of a toy is to grade it. Collectors use a scale of one to ten, with one being the poorest example and ten being the best. Grading toys is subjective. Experienced sellers frequently overgrade the condition of the objects they are selling while individuals with little collecting experience often overgrade the condition of their toys by two to three grades. When grading, it is best to take a conservative approach, that is, undergrade rather than overgrade.

Condition and value are linked. The value of an object increases exponentially as its condition increases. At higher grades, such as near mint and mint, a jump in grade can easily double the value of an object.

OPPOSITE: This Fred Flintstone molded plastic bank is one of a series of banks based on characters from Hanna-Barbera's *The Flintstones* television series.

Tootsietoy first offered this Buck Rogers Battle Cruiser for sale in 1937. It also is found in a yellow and red paint scheme. The toy was one of three different Buck Rogers spaceships made by Tootsietoy. All three had pulleys on top so they could be pushed back and forth on a string. Because of its paint loss, collectors would classify this toy in fair to good condition.

This Bing 12-inch long, lithograph tin, clockwork limousine, circa 1915, is in fine to very fine condition. Toy collectors are more forgiving of wear on pre-1920 toys.

This Dinky, DY-27 1957 Chevrolet Blair Sports Coupe has been graded in excellent condition due to its "like new" appearance and no evidence of wear until inspected with a loupe.

Consider using the following condition scale:

C-1 Parts Toy. A toy from which parts can be salvaged to be used in the repair and restoration of another toy.

C-2 Poor. The toy shows extensive damage and/or wear and may be missing major parts.

C-3 Fair. The toy exhibits signs of heavy use and wear at first glance and can be missing minor parts.

C-4 Good. The toy has visible surface damage and minimal display value. Costs to repair the toy will not be recovered when the restoration is completed.

C-5 Very Good. An observer has to look hard to find minor signs of use. Referred to by collectors as a "lovingly played with toy."

C-6 Fine. Age and wear issues spotted only upon close inspection.

C-7 Very Fine. Although exhibiting minimal wear, the toy has aged and mellowed and, hence, has lost its "like new" appearance.

C-8 Excellent. The toy has retained its like new appearance. Minor surface problems may be evident upon very close inspection.

C-9 Near Mint. The toy still has most of its assembly line luster. There are no detectable problems on the toy's visual surfaces.

C-10 Mint. The toy appears as though it had just left the assembly line. It is flawless.

When grading a toy, hold or look at it from arm's length. Arm's length is the average distance from which one views an object on a shelf or in a cabinet. The display potential of a toy is also a

MIB, mint-in-box, usually refers to a post-1945 toy in C9 condition, such as the Alexander 14" Caroline doll, #1305, from 1962. NRFB, never removed from the box, is a C10 toy.

value key, since collectors place a premium on toys that display well.

If there is noticeable damage when holding an object at arm's length, grade it at C-4 or lower. If there is no visible surface damage, grade it at C-6 or above.

The assumption thus far has been that the toy is complete. If the toy is incomplete, grade it below C-4.

If the toy is accompanied by its period box, the box is graded separately using the same "C" scale. The same applies to toys sold in blister packs.

The Big Three Primary Value Factors

Beginning in the mid-1980s, condition, scarcity, and desirability became the three primary criteria for determining value. In the 1980s and throughout most of the 1990s, condition slightly outweighed the other two in importance. In recent years, the pendulum has swung toward desirability.

Condition

Condition increased in importance as more and more collectors entered the toy arena in the 1970s and 1980s. Collection size gave way to collection quality as the benchmark used to define a major collection.

Most mid-twentieth century collectors focused on the toy. They paid little attention to the box and other packaging in which the toy was sold. This shifted significantly in the 1980s when the concept of MIB, mint-in-box, was introduced. This led to collectors eagerly seeking toys with their period boxes.

Prior to the late 1970s, most toy collections were comprised of toys manufactured from the mid- to late-nineteenth century until the late 1930s. When collectors began collecting post-1945 era toys in the early 1980s, they also started acquiring new examples as they appeared on the market. They preferred to buy the toy new rather than at an increased price when it appeared on the secondary market.

The buying and hoarding of new toy products resulted in the condition grade of NRFB, never removed from the box. Some collectors no longer want toys that exhibit any sign of play. Difficulties arise when collectors try to extend the NRFB condition mentality to pre-1980s toys.

Kids typically threw dime store "civilian" cast-iron figures into a box for storage. Because of this and other types of rough play, finding dimestore figures in excellent or better condition is difficult.

Scarcity Scale

Assumption: Toy is in C-6 condition or better

S-1: Extremely Common. The toy can be acquired in a matter of days or weeks.

S-2: Common. The toy can be acquired in a few weeks or months

S-3: Hard to Find. The toy can be acquired in a few months or a year.

S-4: Scarce. An example appears on the market once every few years.

S-5: Very Scarce. An example appears on the market once or twice in a decade

Scarcity can apply to form, such as this cast-iron truck, or to condition, i.e., how often is the form found in each condition level. Scarcity is something collectors learn through personal observation and interaction. It is subjective.

Scarcity

There are no rare toys anymore. Rarity is a concept whose time has passed. Toys have been mass-produced for a long time, and their individual survival rate is far higher than most collectors are willing to admit.

The Internet, especially eBay, turned the world of scarcity upside down. Prior to the Internet, collectors talked about only three, four, five, etc., known examples of rare items. Today, this number of examples can appear for sale on the Internet in a month or a year.

A subtle distinction has to be made. When discussing scarcity, collectors are referring to the number of examples found in C-6 condition or better. The older the toy, the harder it is to find an example in C-6 condition or better. For this reason, collectors use scarcity as a value consideration far more often for pre-1940 toys than they do for post-1945 toys.

In the twenty-first century, collectors now assume every toy is common. They do not accept scarcity until it is proven.

Desirability

What happens when you have a very scarce toy in mint condition and no buyer? The answer is, there is no value. There is no value without a buyer. In the twenty-first century, desirability has replaced condition as the primary value determinate.

The old assumption was that every toy had an intrinsic value that transcended generations. It was believed that value rested in the toy itself and that the value would remain or even increase over the generations. This is no longer true. Each toy

Louis Marx & Company introduced its lithograph tin, Walking Popeye toy in 1932. Because Popeye remains a strong favorite among comic character collectors, prices for Popeye toys continue to rise.

must stand the test of time with each new generation of collectors.

As the collecting market expanded in the 1980s and 1990s, new collectors faced a growing number of choices with respect to what and how to collect. Niche collecting became the order of the day. Further, younger collectors began concentrating on the toys with which they grew up and played, not those that belonged to their parents, grandparents, and great-grandparents.

Desirability was a leading factor in creating today's trendy secondary marketplace. The value of a toy now needs to be examined on a yearly rather than a multi-year or decade basis. Market shifts can and do occur in a matter of months. Today's popular toy may be tomorrow's dud.

Secondary Values

While condition, scarcity, and desirability head the list of what determines the secondary market value of toys, they are by no means the only factors. Many factors play a role in determining the secondary value of toys.

Complete toy

The definition of a complete toy changed radically at the end of the twentieth century. Previously, a complete toy was a toy that contained all of its parts. (Old-time collectors still use this definition.) After 1960, especially with respect to action figures, the number of pieces accompanying a toy increased. Children that played with these toys often commingled the parts. A new burden fell on toy collectors—knowing which parts came with which toys.

In order for this Alexander 11" Pamela gift set from 1962–63 to be considered complete, it must have the period box, the doll, two replacement wigs, tagged ballerina outfit, two additional outfits, and all the accessories.

As emphasis shifted to the period box, especially for toys manufactured after 1960, a complete toy began to consist of a toy with all its parts plus its box. It did not take long for collectors to recognize that the box was not enough. Many toys also came with protective packaging, instructions, and advertising literature. The definition of completeness was quickly expanded to include this material.

Complete Toy Components

Toys
Accessories
Period box or blister pack
Protective packaging in the box
Advertising, instructions, and other paper ephemera
Shipping box in which the boxed toy or blister packed toy came (extreme cases)

The availability of the box for Marx's 1934 Joe Penner and His Duck Goo Goo enhances the toy's displayability. The better the artwork on a box, the more it contributes to the overall value of the toy. Penner's favorite burlesque line was "Wanna buy a duck?"

Today a toy is complete only if it includes every component it had when it came off the assembly line.

In a few extreme cases, the box in which the boxed toy came also adds value. Toy trains set collectors want the set box as well as all the pieces in the set to have their boxes. The key is the surface image and information on the shipping box. If the image is highly graphic and/or there is information about the toy not found on the individual toy box, then the shipping box adds to the toy's value.

Period box

Collectors value anything that enhances the display quality of a toy. A period box with great graphics or containing manufacturer, play, or other information not found on the toy achieves this goal.

In many cases, the box graphics have more charm and display value

than the toy itself. The graphic box art on post-War War II battery operated and lithograph tin toys and Mattel's box graphics for Barbie accessories are examples.

In some cases, the box was part of the toy's play value. The box for the Amos and Andy lithographed tin toy taxi served as its garage.

Period boxes are graded using the same C-1 to C-10 condition scale that is used for toys. It is quite possible to find a C-8 toy with a C-4 box. A C-5 or C-6 box traditionally adds 20 to 40 percent to the value of a toy. There are even instances when the value of the box exceeds that of the toy. Determining the added value of the box is highly subjective.

Crossover value

If value is in the eyes of the collector, it is possible for toys to have more than one value. The key is to determine the number of potential collectors for a specific toy and then ask what value each collector would assign to that toy.

Use Hasbro's G.I. Joe Action Pilot Official Space Capsule as an example. The G.I. Joe collector is the most obvious potential collector. However, the capsule also has appeal to the astronaut collector, the space race collector, the specialist G.I. Joe

This Ideal 15" Mary Hartline doll has crossover appeal to early television show memorabilia collectors, Chicago-area collectors, circus collectors, and specialized personality doll collectors as well as to the general doll collector. Mary Hartline starred on ABC's *Super Circus* from January 1949 to December 1955. Chicago's WERN-TV produced the show.

Hasbro's 1966 G.I. Joe Action Pilot Official Space Capsule and Authentic Space Suit contained a floating space capsule, sliding canopy, control panel, retro pack, communications plug-in, authentic space suit, astronaut helmet, space gloves and boots, and a soundtrack recording of an actual Mercury Flight. Most complete units in toy collections have been reassembled by collectors.

accessories only collector, the period icon toy collector, and the period illustration collector (the box has great graphics). Each of these potential collectors values the toy differently.

Almost every toy has three or more potential buyers. Many have six or more. Once a collector learns to look for them, he or she begins recognizing them. In time, identifying the crossover potential of toys becomes instinctual.

The end result is that when someone asks about the secondary market value of a toy, the question that needs to be asked before answering is, "value to what collector?"

Period paint

Many nineteenth- and early-twentieth-century cast-iron, tin, and wood toys were painted. In spite of the modern trend to restore toys to their "like new" appearance, there is a dedicated corps of collectors who place value on a toy retaining its period paint. Mechanical bank collectors are perhaps the most extreme.

Determining the percentage of remaining period paint is entirely subjective. Yet, collectors and dealers make differentiations in units of 1, not 5 or 10 percent. In toys where period paint is critical to value, value increases exponentially.

At the moment, there are no professional toy grading services. Collectors of toys for which period paint is a value consideration have been discussing this possibility. Collectors have been deterred due to the need to encapsulate any graded toy so it can no longer be touched.

The sum of the parts

Mathematics teaches that the whole is equal to the sum of the parts. This is not always the case when it comes to toys. There are times when the sum of the parts is greater than the whole. As previously noted there are cases when the period box may be worth more than the toy itself.

The more parts a toy has, the more likely parts will be lost through play. A toy with all its parts is the basic unit of value. If a toy is missing parts, its

If a dealer sold the four tiny television cameras and game board individually, he would receive more money than if he sold the game as a complete unit. Collectors often pay a premium for missing or lost parts.

Many doll series, such as Nancy Ann Storybook dolls, used the same body. Different outfits created the variations. Occasionally, manufacturers did make subtle changes to the bodies of doll series that were produced for an extended period of time.

value diminishes. If the part is a strong component of display, the diminished value may well exceed 50 percent of the toy's value.

Toy parts can and often do have individual value. Some dealers will even break a complete toy apart and sell the parts individually to enhance their return.

Variants

Many manufacturers change the accessories of a specific toy during an extended manufacturing period. Another common practice is to change the color or paint scheme, which leads to variants.

It is common to visit an advanced collector and find six or more variants for a single toy in his or her collection. This requires a sophisticated knowledge of what was produced. Manufacturers usually do not disclose this information. As a result, collectors are never certain that they have "all" the examples of a single toy.

Foreign licensing increases this collecting conundrum. Many American-based toys are also licensed overseas. In today's age of global col-

lecting, many collections include foreign-licensed examples. Further, the accessories found in foreign-licensed examples often differ from those found in American-licensed products.

Variants can haunt the toy collector. It is almost impossible to rest assured that a collection contains all known variants.

Toys as investments

Some high-end toy collectors and dealers have attempted to create "investment" grade toys, toys they tout as having universal collecting value. They rely on the premise that a new generation of collectors will continually replace older collectors who leave the market. In truth, the investment toy market is speculative and manipulative. There is plenty of cause for doubt that today's investment grade toys will stand the test of time.

Several toy collecting categories, such as nineteenth- and early-twentieth-century painted tin, mechanical banks, early pressed-steel vehicles, and Disneyana, have been touted as investment grade toys. However, it is critical to understand that this does not apply to all toys in these categories, but only to the top 50 to 150 toys in the category, referred to by collectors as the "high-end."

Investment grade toys are bought and sold as commodities, not as something with which to play or something to love. It is critical to remember that the value paid for these toys is not intrinsic in the toy but in the mindset of the individuals doing the purchasing. Value remains only so long as future buyers continue to accept this value structure.

Condition grade and investment grade are linked. Investment grade for a toy manufactured in the twenty-first century is C-10. That is, a toy from this period must appear to have just come off the assembly line in order to be considered investment grade. No matter how far back one goes, investment grade never falls below C-6.

It also is critical to understand that many have serious questions about the investment grade potential of any toy manufactured after 1963. The survival rate and hoarding of toys from this era suggests there will never come a point when demand exceeds supply in the long-term.

The Fischer Quints, born in September 1963, were the first set of quintuplets born in the United States. Do you remember them? I was a twenty-one at the time, and I did not remember who they were until I researched them on the Internet. Alexander produced this set of 8" Fischer Quints in 1964.

Investment Grade By Date

1850 to 1920	C-6
1920 to 1945	C-7
1945 to 1963	C-8
1963 to 1980	C-9
1980 to Present	C-10

Tertiary Values

As if the issue of toy value was not complicated enough, there is a third set of factors that influence the value of a toy. Although minor in their impact, these factors do need to be taken into consideration.

Most pre-1920 automobiles in fine or better condition are viewed as investment grade by collectors. This French Jouet de Paris, painted tin, clockwork race car with rubber tires, circa 1900, is valued over $2,000.

Is this 1950s dime store Indian worth more if the maker, in this case, Barclay, is known? The answer is yes. Further, when accompanied by other Barclay Indian figurines from the same era, its value is enhanced further.

Regional and local value

Prior to 1945, many toys were sold regionally, not nationally. Regionally sold toys tend to have a greater value in the region in which they were originally sold than elsewhere.

Many collectors focus on toys made in their locality; for instance, the bulk of the collectors for Sun Rubber toys are found in Akron-Barberton, Ohio. American collectors are often driven by local or regional pride.

The national promotion and sale of toys is directly linked to the arrival of national television. While some national distribution occurred through Montgomery Ward, Sears, and five and dime stores, television was responsible for creating national demand. Once large national toy chain stores arrived on the scene, all toys had a national focus.

The oldest or the first

Some American collectors still place value on owning the oldest or the first model of any toy made. Such claims are often difficult to prove because of the lack of manufacturing records.

Historically, collectors attributed added value to the oldest or first example of a toy. Today's collectors may question this approach, but this sacred cow always remains in the back of their minds.

Provenance

Value is added to a toy if it belonged to a famous

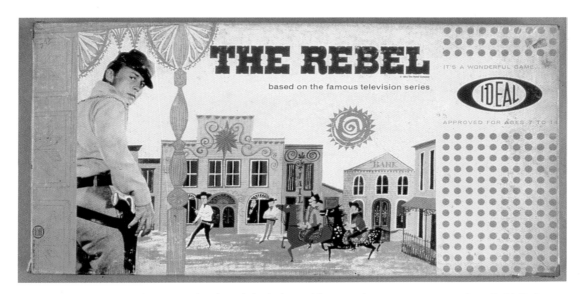

Johnny Cash recorded the theme song for *The Rebel*, which aired from October 4, 1959 to September 17, 1961. Do you know who played Johnny Yuma, the ex-Confederate? Do you even remember the show?

person or was once part of a famous collection. Consideration must be given to the celebrity of the person and the collection, and how long that person will be remembered in history. A teddy bear belonging to President Theodore Roosevelt is an example of a toy whose provenance is eternal. A toy from the collection of a famous collector only has value as long as there are collectors who remember that individual.

Wise collectors should constantly question the value of provenance. Like so many values, it is subject to the whims of the market. Collectors are aware that fame is fleeting.

Research

Another old value adage is "the more you know about a toy, the greater its value." Information does increase a toy's value. Most collectors consider

Six Questions Every Collector Wants to Know about a Toy

1. Who designed it?
2. Who made it?
3. When was it made?
4. In what variations was it made?
5. How many were made?
6. How long was it made?

themselves lucky if they know when a toy was made and who manufactured it. Any additional information is considered a bonus.

Memory

Memory is a value, although many toy collectors do not even consider it when evaluating a toy. They prefer to think the next generation will remember and love their toys with the same intensity they exhibit. Recent market pricing trends are proving them wrong.

One-generation value

In the twenty-first century, a critical value question to ask is, "What's going to happen to the value of a generation's toys when that generation dies?" The simple truth is that toy memory is not eternal. We have reached the point where it is more likely for certain groups of toys to be found in museums than private collections.

Do any of the following sound familiar? Arcade, Buddy L, Hopalong Cassidy, Hubley, the Yellow Kid? If you cannot identify them, why would you collect objects associated with them?

Many traditional toy collectors are having a hard time accepting the fact that future generations of toy collectors may not have the same collecting interests as past and present generations. A collector of Transformers toys may not care one iota about cast-iron toys.

Mattel manufactured a wide range of toys in addition to Barbie. Mattel toys, such as this 1962 VAC-U-FORM and Creepy Crawler toys, from the 1960s and 1970s have become highly desirable to the generations who grew up with them.

The real value of this Mattel Woody Woodpecker pull string, talking doll is only what he is worth to you. If you do not care, the doll has no value in spite of what a price guide says.

are generic, non-licensed toys, most of which fall outside the collecting sphere.

What Is the Real Price?

In the final analysis, there is only one value that concerns the collector—what he or she is willing to pay for an object. There is no sale without his or her willingness to buy.

Most collectors do not buy with the expectation of reselling. They buy to build and enhance their collections. They expect to retain their latest purchase for a lifetime or until they tire of the collection. Value rests with the importance the object has assumed in their collection.

In the 1990s, analysts of pricing trends in toy collecting began to notice a significant decline in the value of many toy-collecting categories, ranging from cast-iron toys to 1950s television cowboy memorabilia. At first, the trend was most noticeable for commonly found toys. Eventually, it spread to the above-average and even high-end toys in some categories.

Few modern toys have exhibited "decade" staying power, remaining on the toy shelf for ten years or longer. Licensed toys associated with movies and personalities come and go within a matter of months. Many of the toys that do survive

Always carefully examine your new aquisition to determine if they have sustained any damage.

CHAPTER SEVEN

IS IT GENUINE?

T rust is an important element in buying antique and collectible toys. The collector expects the seller to properly represent the object he or she is selling. *Caveat emptor*, let the buyer beware, is the principle that governs all sales in the antiques and collectibles field. In simplest terms, *caveat emptor* places the burden on the buyer to know what you are buying, not on the seller to know what he or she is selling.

Learning how to distinguish period pieces from reproductions, copycats, fantasy items, and fakes is an essential lesson in your toy-collecting education. It is also important to understand how to spot restoration and repairs, both of which can have a negative impact on value. Well-documented information is key; distrust and discount all information that appears speculative, hypothetical, and a guesstimate.

To become a savvy toy collector you must take to heart the old adage of practice makes perfect. Mistakes will happen, especially when first starting to collect. Try not to get too upset, but be certain to learn from them. They are the tuition you pay to become an advanced, serious collector.

The process of separating period toys from reproductions, copycats, fantasy items, and of

OPPOSITE: The Merrymakers mouse band.

Is the costume on this Horsman, 25-inch high, Mama Baby, doll period or a later addition? The doll has been redressed. Doll collectors are extremely tolerant of redressing. Period clothing usually represents only 10 to 15 percent of an antique doll's value.

fakes and of recognizing restoration and repairs is called "authentication." The same rules that apply to authenticating toys apply to all antiques and collectibles. Once you have learned them, you can use them universally.

Terminology

Correct terminology is necessary to properly authenticate a toy. There are words in the antiques and collectibles lexicon that are meaningless or have hidden meaning. The words *genuine*, *real*, and *original* are so ambiguous that they are essentially empty terms. If you are looking at a toy, it is genuine. It also is real and original. Genuine, real, and original are terms that can be used to fool buyers into paying premium prices for reproductions, copycats, fantasy items, and fakes.

Style is an example of a word with hidden meaning. Essentially "style" means a later copy. "In the style of," when applied to a manufacturer, means that while it

---

Half a Dozen Tips to Consider when Buying a Toy

1. Do not buy what you do not know. Buy only toys that you have researched both history and value.
2. Force yourself to take the time to examine the toy thoroughly. If the lighting is poor, ask permission to take the toy to a location where the lighting is better.
3. Ask questions: (1) Is the toy complete? (2) Has any restoration or repainting been done? (3) Are there condition problems I did not see? (4) When was the toy made? (5) Did the toy have a box? If the seller cannot answer your questions to your satisfaction, walk away.
4. Do not accept the seller's word regarding scarcity and condition. Most sellers overestimate both. Make your own judgment.
5. Do not buy without a receipt that indicates the seller's name, an address at which he or she can be reached, and a phone number and/or an e-mail address. Insist the seller indicate the date the toy was made on the receipt. If there is a question later, this is critical to making a case for having your purchase money refunded.

6. Do not hesitate to comparison shop. Remember, all toys were mass-produced. Their survival rate is far greater than most collectors and sellers assume.

When buying any battery-operated toy first check the battery compartment for rust. Second insert the proper batteries to make certain the toy is in working order. Most wires cannot be repaired without taking the toy apart, something that can cause irreversible damage.

A toy, such as a lithograph tin automobile, has to have no alternations or changes to be considered period. The toy must be "assembly-line" pure.

may be similar to toys made by a particular manufacturer, the toy is not by that manufacturer.

Period is the term for a toy that was made during the time period when the toy was first produced and which has not been altered in any manner except through play. As period toys become collectible and often unaffordable to the average collector, later examples of the toy are made to fill collectors' demand.

A *reissue* is a toy made from the same die, mold, or printing plate used to create the period toy. Collectors often fail to consider the question, "What happened to the period molds?" Many assume that they are destroyed,

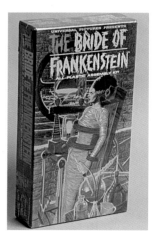

but manufacturers are aware that dies, molds, and printing plates are valuable assets. When a company is purchased, these assets transfer to the new owner. Often all that is required to put the toy back into production is to move the necessary dies, molds, and printing plates back to the assembly line. If a company goes into bankruptcy and its assets are sold, die, molds, and printing plates can wind up in private hands.

Reissues are extremely difficult to identify. Ideally, when the manufacturer reissues a toy, it should identify the toy by making an easily recognizable change in the toy's design. In reality it happens in less than half of cases.

The best way to spot reissues is to be suspicious of any twenty-five years old or older toy that appears brand new. A near mint toy with near mint packaging is another clue. Collectors' clubs often alert the collecting community when a reissue is spotted. Also, talk with other collectors.

A *reproduction* is an exact copy of a period toy. When placed side by side, it is extremely difficult to distinguish one from the other. There are usually subtle differences that distinguish a reproduction from a period toy. The size may be slightly different. The colors may not

LEFT: What happened to period production molds or plates? Most manufacturers retained them. Period molds and plates were used for this Playing Mantis's 1997 reproduction of this Aurora *The Bride of Frankenstein* model kit. RIGHT: This American Character 17" Sweet Sue "Sunday Best" walker doll was first produced in 1952. Her body and costume are "period."

The Toy Museum in East Aurora, New York, home of Fisher-Price, issues a reproduction Fisher-Price toy for its annual ToyFest celebration. This Fisher-Price Hot Dog Wagon was done in 2001 in celebration of the ToyFest Fifteenth Anniversary. The toy is marked in several locations so it cannot be confused with the period piece.

be an exact match. Interior manufacturing details may differ. The period piece often shows signs of use that are missing on the reproduction.

A *copycat* is a stylistic reproduction of a period piece. Although it may appear identical to a period toy at first glance, the differences are quickly apparent. There may be changes in shape, color and decoration scheme, and size.

When a copycat appears on the market during the initial period of a toy's production, it is called a *knock-off*. Knock-offs are common. Usually a knock-off is a generic version of a licensed-product toy. During the period of popularity of The Mighty Morphin Power Rangers, knock-off mask and costume sets flooded the market.

A *fantasy item* is a toy that mimics the design of a period toy, but the shape, form, and/or decorative motif is different. Fantasy toys most often appear when there is a toy revival, such as the *Star Wars* craze. Many of these toys are highly romanticized, relying on collectors' devotion to motivate them to buy.

Toys issued as collectors' club commemoratives and convention memorabilia are also described as fantasy items, even though these have collector value. They differ from period toys in that they were manufactured later. The standard rule of thumb is that copycats and fantasy items lack the quality of period pieces. While poor quality may distinguish some copycats and fantasy items, it is a mistake to assume all are poor quality. Some are better made than the original period toys.

Reproductions, copycats, and fantasy items, like reissues, usually start out life honestly. However, unscrupulous dealers may remove their identifying marks, artificially age them, and try to pass them off as period pieces.

LEFT: This Super Robotic Rangers Play Set is a Chinese knock-off of *The Mighty Morphin Power Rangers*. It sold for ninety-nine cents, far below the price charged for a similar licensed example. RIGHT: Matchbox has done hundreds of special issue cars, for example for the New York Toy Fairs and Matchbox collector conventions, over the past several decades. Many appear for sale on eBay shortly after issue.

A *fake* is an item deliberately meant to deceive. The manufacturer produced it to fool collectors. The wholesaler sold it to dealers who clearly planned to mislabel it when offering it for sale.

Fakes divide into two groups, one-of-a-kind and mass-produced. One-of-a-kind fakes are encountered primarily by collectors of wooden and other primitive "folk" toys. Most fake toys are mass-produced reproductions, made deliberately to deceive.

Because reissues, reproductions, copycats, fantasy items, and most fakes are mass-produced, their arrival in the toy marketplace is quickly noticed. A toy that you have never seen before, or in a condition in which you are not used to seeing, should be cause for suspicion. Be skeptical of dealers who explain the arrival as a "warehouse find." "Warehouse find" is a marketing ploy used to introduce reissues, reproductions, copycats, fantasy items, and fakes into the marketplace.

Common Sense Rules

It does not take sophisticated equipment to spot most reissues, reproductions, copycats, fantasy items, and fakes. It takes only common sense and practice, and can be learned quickly by most novices.

The ten common sense rules that follow are a quick course in becoming an accomplished authenticator. Practice is an important element in improving and perfecting your abilities. Even the most experienced collector continues to hone his or her skills. Authentication is a lifelong learning process.

Consider each rule an alarm bell. When the alarm bell rings, pay attention. Take a breath, slow down, and begin the authentication process.

Rule 1: If it looks new, assume it is new

Toys are designed to be played with, and as time takes its toll, older toys are expected to have signs of age and use. Collectors use the term *patina* to describe the overall look of a toy that has softened and mellowed with age. Patina results from a reaction of the toy's surface with the chemicals and dirt in the air.

Natural aging may result in crazing, the appearance of crackling or small cracks in the surface paint of a toy, or other minor surface flaws. Most collectors accept this. They also distinguish it from other damage caused by wear.

This Remco Raphel model *Teenage Mutant Ninja Turtles* baseball glove still retains its "new" look and label. It has never been used for play.

When examining a toy, think about how it was used for play. Put your hands on it as though you were playing with it. If possible, play with it. Pay close attention to how the parts interact with the playing surface and your hands. Now look for wear. Is it where it should be?

Unscrupulous dealers who artificially age reproductions, copycats, and fakes often do not pay attention to where the wear should occur. They just rough up the toy. When you spot wear on a toy that does not make sense, be skeptical. There should be appropriate wear on both the visible portions of the toy and on the interior surface.

"If it looks new, it is new" is not an easy rule to follow. The thrill of finding a period toy in near mint condition almost always overrides common sense. Train yourself to avoid this.

Rule 2: Examine all toys in natural or the best available light

Examine a toy in your living room or basement. Now take it outside and look at it in natural sunlight. Do not be surprised when you notice far more condition problems than you did when examining the toy inside.

Fluorescent and other interior lighting has a strong tendency to change the color of objects. When color is critical to identifying a variant, only trust natural sunlight.

When examining a toy in natural sunlight or in any light, stand off to one side of the light source so the light rakes across the toy's surface. Move the toy up, down, and around. Again, you will be surprised at how much you now see that you did not see initially.

Our eyes want a toy to appear as it should. As a result, our eyes often visually correct problems when one views a toy as one normally would. The key is to rotate the toy so you are not looking at it in its normal position. Unaccustomed to seeing the toy in these new positions, your eyes no longer deceive you.

Rule 3: Examine all sides

How many sides does a toy have? Since toys are three dimensional, the standard answer is six—front, back, left side, right side, top and bottom. In fact, toys have seven sides. The seventh side is the inside, the most important side when authenticating a toy. The aging and wear inside needs to be consistent with what is found on the outside.

A second part of this rule is that if the toy comes apart, take it apart and examine each part individually. Two corollaries to this rule are (1) if you take it apart, you had better be able to put it back together again and (2) ask the dealer's permission before doing this.

When examining a toy, pay close attention to how the individual parts interact with each other. Surfaces that rub together must show signs of wear. Metal rubbing against metal leaves a wear groove.

Dealers with nothing to hide will have no problem with you closely examining a toy. In fact, they often are more than glad to participate in the process. Again, if the lighting is bad, ask the dealer's permission to take the toy to a better light source.

Be suspicious of dealers who do not allow you to handle a toy or protest you examining it too closely. The moment you feel a dealer is trying to hide something, walk away.

Dave Bausch and the author examine the Kingsbury Golden Arrow racer outside. By raking light across the toy, they are able to see damage that was not readily apparent when they viewed the car inside David's house.

Rule 4: Check for consistency

All parts of a toy should be made with the same quality of workmanship. When you spot a part that does not exhibit this quality, chances are strong that it has been replaced.

Collectors study how toys were made. Manufacturing techniques vary over time. A toy supposedly made in the late nineteenth century should have characteristics associated with that manufacturing time period and not the mid-twentieth century.

If a toy is symmetrical, mentally draw a line down the center of the toy and begin a left to right checklist comparison. If a toy is asymmetrical, look for consistency in the manufacture of its parts. Consistency is about harmony; everything should be as it is meant to be.

There are exceptions to all rules. The conductor's hands on the famous Toonerville Trolley lithograph tin toy have no lithography on them. When you first examine the toy, the inconsistency is striking. However, as you examine other examples, the inconsistency is constant. In this case, the inconsistency is consistant.

1. Feel the surface. Period toys have smooth surfaces, later toys have rough surfaces.

2. Study the joints. Period toys have tight joints, later toys do not. If you can slip a piece of paper through the joint, it is not a good sign.

3. Check the finishing. Period toys have all flanges filed off and no sign of where the toy was broken off from the casting gate. Later toys often have rough edges, especially on wheels, and a clear indication of where the casting gate was located.

4. If the surface paint looks new, chances are the toy is a reproduction or copycat.

5. If there is interior rust and it is orange and flaky, be suspicious. Older rust is a deep dark red and greasy to the touch.

The Hubley Manufacturing Company made quality cast-iron toys. Joints fit tightly. Surfaces are smooth. These characteristics and more are visible on this Auto Express, open body truck made circa 1910.

Rule 5: Beware of apologies

The more a dealer apologizes for the flaws in a toy, the more suspicious you need to be. When a toy is a reproduction, copycat, fantasy item, or fake or has been restored or repaired, there are usually multiple clues to assist you.

A questioning mind is only the first step. Always

When determining the authenticity of this Fisher-Price, check a Fisher-Price reference book to determine what materials were used to produce it. Use this information as a checklist to examine the toy.

inquire if the dealer is aware of any restoration or repair, does he or she know if the toy has ever been reissued, reproduced, or copied, and will he or she provide you with a receipt indicating the time when he or she believes the toy was manufactured.

When an answer sounds stock and pat, you need to dig deeper. Most dealers are honest and should provide accurate and plausible answers to the questions you ask.

Rule 6: Beware of bargains

Every collector loves to tell about the bargains he or she found during collecting. Collectors who hunt with patience and determination will find them.

However, a bargain price also is an alarm trigger. Reissues, reproductions, copycats, fantasy items, and fakes often are sold at bargain prices. The low price is an incentive to encourage a quick purchase without first properly examining the piece.

Take advantage of bargains when you find them. Not every alarm bell that goes off is a true alarm. There are false alarms. When you have determined the alarm is false, consider buying the toy.

Rule 7: Create a construction, color, and form vocabulary in your mind

Think cast-iron vehicles, think 1920s and1930s. Think die-cast vehicles, think post-1960s. Think pink and black, think 1950s. Think avocado, golden harvest, and rust, think 1970s. Think streamlined design, think 1940s through 1960s. Think boxlike design, think late-twentieth century. These differences are known as collecting vocabulary.

You create these vocabularies by handling period toys. Pay attention to how the toy was made, the color tones used to paint the toy, the designs found on the toy's surface, and the size and shape of the toy. Toys produced at the same time tend to follow standard formulas. Manufacturers copy one another, and few dare to be different. The market reacts to what is popular.

Developing construction, color, pattern, and shape vocabularies takes time. It also takes memory. You need to train yourself to remember

If you see the Milton Bradley Fess Parker Trail Blazers boxed board game for sale at a flea market or antiques mall for five dollars or less, chances are the game has one or more missing parts.

No two collectors look at a toy the same way. As a result, each sees things the other may miss. This is why a second set of eyes is extremely helpful when authenticating toys.

what you have seen in the past and constantly compare it to what you are seeing in the present. In this way you can train your eye to recognize items that just don't look right and may be fakes.

Rule 8: Create a file on reissues, reproductions, copycats, fantasy items, and fakes in your area of collecting interest

Identify the manufacturers and wholesalers who make and distribute reissues, reproductions, copycats, fantasy items, and fakes. Write for their catalogs. Acquire examples for your own collection and study them.

There is no reference book that provides a checklist of past reissues, reproductions, copycats, fantasy items, and fakes. However, there is an Internet site, www.repronews.com that tracks the "reproduction" market as a whole. It offers a wealth of toy information and can be a valuable resource.

Rule 9: Handle and study good examples in your area of collecting interest

There is no substitute for handling the real thing. Handling objects allows you to create a mental

The artwork, form (1954 Buick), and color scheme of this Asian manufactured lithograph tin, Minister Delux friction car suggest a 1950s manufacturing date. However, the car was made later. Remember, there are exceptions to every rule.

vocabulary concerning the proper weight and surface texture of a period object. Once you have familiarized yourself with a period toy, you will never have trouble separating it from a reissue, reproduction, copycat, fantasy item, or fake.

Where can you study toys? The best source is your local historical society. Most local historical societies have toy collections. The National Museum of Play in Rochester, New York, is an excellent destination. The reference librarian at your closest public library has access to a museum reference source that will help you locate toy collections in your immediate vicinity.

Toy auctions are an excellent place to handle period toys. In fact, the auctioneer actually will encourage you to handle the toys. Whenever possible, attend the preview of a cataloged toy auction. Compare the catalog description with the toy you are handling. Chances are other collectors will be doing the same. If you see someone you recognize, work together and exchange views.

One of the best places to view toys is at the home of a private collector. Never turn down an invitation

Tips to Consider when Buying a Boxed Board Game

1. Is it complete? The instruction sheet or instructions printed inside the lid or on the game board usually contain a list of parts. Game parts get exchanged through play. Make certain the pieces found in the box are the correct ones.
2. Is it possible to buy a second incomplete game to get the parts necessary to make an initial incomplete game complete?
3. The cover image and condition of the box are critical to value. Most boxed board games are displayed closed.
4. Generic games, e.g., Candy Land, Monopoly, Scrabble, etc., have little collector value.
5. Boxed board games survive in large quantities, especially those manufactured after 1945. Prices

realized on eBay are a good barometer of their worth.

The play instructions for this *Charlie's Angels* boxed board game contain a list of the game parts. Take the time to count the parts to make certain the game is complete before purchasing it.

from a major collector. When visiting, ask the collector if his collection has reissues, reproductions, copycats, fantasy items, and fakes. If it does, and it probably will, ask him to explain to you how they differ from the period toys in the collection.

The Unwritten Rule: Share your knowledge and spread the word

If you buy a reissue, reproduction, copycat, fantasy item, or fake thinking it is a period toy, do not send your mistake back into the marketplace. Use it to educate. Show the toy to others and explain how and why you know it is not period.

When you spot a dealer falsely selling period toys, tell other potential buyers. If you see this occurring at a flea market, antiques mall, or antiques show, report it to the manager for the good of the entire toy-collecting community.

Restoration and Repairs

Restoration is used to describe a toy that has been returned to the same appearance it had when it was made. All signs of aging and wear have been

Can you spot the restoration on this Hafner Touring Car? If not, look again. Spotting restoration in photographs is extremely difficult. Remember, the key is handling the object.

removed. The restored toy may contain new parts. The key is that it appears brand new.

The toy-collecting community is continually debating the issue of how much restoration is acceptable. In the case of late-nineteenth and early-twentieth century painted tin toys, pressed-steel vehicles, and pedal cars, total restoration is rapidly becoming the accepted norm.

A *repair* is something done to a toy to make a toy whole again. Repairs can be made with period or new parts. Again, the toy-collecting community debates the issue of whether or not repairs should be done so they are not noticeable or whether the repair should be done but be evident.

Your eyes are the best means for spotting restoration and repairs. Examining the toy in the dark using an ultraviolet light can also illuminate changes in the reflection of the light off the surface—which signals that the toy may have been restored or repaired.

There is no law that requires a dealer to reveal any restoration or repair when selling a toy. The burden is on the buyer to ask and examine.

CHAPTER EIGHT

MANAGING YOUR COLLECTION

As your toy collection grows, you are creating a private museum. Few collectors think of their collections in this sense, but it is true. Collectors preserve and record the past, display their collections for themselves and others to enjoy, and take the necessary steps to preserve what they collect for the next generation. This is what historical sites, historical societies, and museums do.

Help is available to teach you some of the important skills of a museum curator. You can contact the American Association for State and Location History (AASLH), 1717 Church Street, Nashville, TN 37203, and ask for a list of their publications and technical leaflets or you can find them on the AASLH website, www.aaslh.org.

The AASLH technical leaflet series began in 1962, but some of the earlier issues are out of print. If you are lucky, a local historical site, society, or museum in your area has a full run. You will shorten your learning curve by months if not years if you spend some time reading through a variety of leaflets.

OPPOSITE: When displaying toys in a cabinet, toy collectors tend to group toys by type. Toy collectors prefer old wooden cabinets because of the "antique" feel over post-1945 Modernist lighted cabinets.

The purchase information for this handmade Felix the Cat walking toy has been lost. In addition, the collector has no recollection of where or how he acquired it. For these reasons, it is critical to catalog toys within a few days or weeks of purchase.

Keeping Proper Records

Many collectors are poor record keepers. It is much more fun to acquire and play with toys than create and maintain the records that document a collection. A simple rule applies—the further you get behind, the less likely you are to ever catch up. The only solution is to keep proper records from the start and take the time to update them as you acquire more toys.

If you are going to keep only one set of records, create an acquisition list, that is, a chronological list of your toy purchases. A simplified acquisition list contains the following elements:

(1) a number assigned to each toy
(2) date of purchase
(3) brief description of the toy
(4) identity of the seller
(5) price paid

Acquisition lists are generally kept in a ledger or computer spreadsheet program.

Ideally you will obtain a sales receipt for each purchase. Write the acquisition number on the sales receipt. A sales receipt should contain the name, address, and other contact information of the seller, the date, a full description of the item, the date the seller believes the item was made, any restoration, repair, or condition issues, the amount paid including the sales tax, and any guarantees made by the seller.

Sales receipts are valuable references and can be kept together in a box or file folder. If using a computer program, make certain to occasionally print out the acquisition file and back it up on a CD or other external unit.

Besides serving as a basic record for a collector, acquisition records also serve two additional purposes. First, they are a starting point for evaluating your toy collection for insurance purposes. Second, should the necessity arise, they are helpful to your heirs in determining the value of the items in your collection.

Another important step in documenting your collection is creating a photographic acquisition record, as well as a written one. A digital camera is very useful for this purpose.

The Catalog Sheet

Acquisition Number: The simplest method is to assign a two-digit year number and a sequential number based on purchases made during the year. For example 07.35 is the thirty-fifth toy purchase made in 2007.

Name: This is the name found on the toy or by which the toy is known among collectors.

Description: Your goal is to describe the toy in enough detail so that another toy collector could easily identify it. Do not forget to include information about the box, packaging, or other items that came with the toy.

Manufacturer and Date of Manufacture: Manufacturing information is often lost, so do not become frustrated if you don't have it. It is highly likely you will discover it later, at which point you can add it. When estimating the date of manufacture, try not to use more than a ten- to fifteen-year time spread, such as 1945–55 or 1920s–30s.

Dimensions: Three measurements are enough— maximum width, depth, and height. Round measurements off to the nearest eighth of an inch. The measurements of the box should be included too.

Condition: First, grade the object using the "C" code. Second, note any condition problems. Third, examine the toy carefully and record any repairs or restoration.

Provenance: There are three types of provenance— previous owners, places where the toy may have been exhibited or illustrated, and auction history.

Research: Indicate the reference books and other sources that contain information about your toy. Make photocopies or print out copies of this information and attach it to the acquisition sheet.

Purchase Information: Repeat the information found in your acquisition book.

Photograph: Photograph the toy you purchased.

Date: Sign, date, and initial the catalog sheet.

Appraisal: This figure represents the replacement value of the toy in the existing market. It should be revisited every five to seven years.

Location: Toy collectors tend to place a toy in a location that quickly becomes permanent, so note the room and location in the room where the toy can be found. If the toy is placed into storage, number the storage units, especially if using generic boxes.

Comments: Occasionally you come across miscellaneous information that simply does not fit elsewhere on the form.

Revision Date: As you become more experienced, your knowledge will increase. Use a revision date as a reminder of the last time you looked at the catalog record.

There is a lot to catalog regarding this Ideal 12" Shirley Temple doll, circa 1958, in the costume worn by Shirley in the movie *Captain January*. Besides information about the doll, the catalog sheet also should contain information about the movie and, ideally, the scene in the movie when she wore this costume.

Cataloging presents you with the opportunity to learn more about the toy you purchased. Your challenge is to view it as fun rather than drudgery. Prior to the advent of the computer, most toy collectors designed a one-page catalog sheet with blank space for the basic catalog information. Today, it is far simpler to use a computer program. Using a spreadsheet program rather than a word processing program will allow you to extract, compare, and analyze information blocks. Although several commercial software programs exist for cataloging objects, there are none which are toy specific, and many provide only a limited amount of space for information. You can design your own spreadsheet so that it contains all the categories essential for your needs and leaves ample space to insert additional information.

As seen on the previous page, the basic catalog sheet should contain the toy's acquisition number, name, description, manufacturer and date of manufacture, dimensions, condition, provenance, research information, photograph, purchase information, and date the form was filled out. Also consider including columns for appraisal data, display and storage location, comments, and revision date.

Store your catalog records numerically by acquisition number. If you want a set of records by toy type, consider duplicating the catalog page and creating a second set of files.

Finally, if you sell a toy, consider passing along your catalog sheet to the purchaser. It will be appreciated.

Displaying Your Collection

Now that the paperwork is finished, let the fun begin. It is time to show off your toy purchases. Remember, you are displaying toys. Therefore, select a display method that allows easy access to your toys so that you can play with them.

There is no single right way to display toys. They can be grouped by type, manufacturer, historical time period, size, color, or graphic value. Use your imagination. The right way to display your toys is the display method that brings you the greatest pleasure.

When displaying toys, there are certain considerations that are essential to ensure their long-term protection. You are a caretaker, responsible for passing along the toy to the next owner in as good or better condition than you received it.

Rapid change in temperature is the greatest threat to toys. Avoid displaying toys near heating and return ducts and on shelving attached to outside walls. Rapid changes in temperature can cause surface paint to crack or fade, glue to loosen, and lithography to blister. If placing your toys in a lighted case, check them once a month to make certain no damage has occurred.

Direct exposure to sunlight is another threat to your toys. Sunlight

Many doll collectors use stands to display their dolls. Make certain you buy a stand that has a plastic tube over the metal arms that extended around the doll's body. Exposed metal can rust if exposed to high humidity. Also, beware of buying a stand that grips the doll too tightly. This can cause damage to the clothing and body.

Collectors love to display toys as they were meant to be used. A toy train platform provides the ideal environment to do this. This method of display can present interesting cleaning challenges.

acts as a bleach, causing colors to fade. The same is true for floodlights, fluorescent lighting, and spotlights. If using these lights, obtain protective shields that reduce their harmful aspects.

Many toy collectors have a bad habit of placing too many toys on wall mounted shelves and on shelving in display cases. Test the weight-bearing load of any wall mounted shelf before placing your toys on it. Check the shelf supports in display cases every three months. If you notice they are coming loose, you have too much weight on the shelf. Also check the balance of your display cases using a level. If you find the case is leaning forward, correct this flaw immediately.

Humidity is another key concern, especially if toys are stored in a basement, attic, or garage. The ideal humidity is about 55 to 60 percent. It also is essential that the humidity remains constant. If necessary, purchase a humidifier or dehumidifier.

It is a good idea to examine your collection on a monthly basis for bugs, especially if displaying boxes, paper lithograph toys, advertising, or other paper ephemera. Cockroaches, mites, silverfish, and other insects thrive on old, damp paper.

Make it a practice to keep your toys clean, using a feather duster or a very soft cloth while avoiding cleaning aids treated with dust-attracting chemicals. You do not want any of these chemicals left behind on your toys' surfaces.

If you hire someone to clean, provide specific instructions on how to handle your toys. Consider providing the cleaning person with a photograph of each display area so that the toys are put back in their exact locations.

If you live in an area that is subject to earthquakes or tornados, there are clays and other substances you can purchase to secure your toys to the display shelves. Take the same precautions if your toys are displayed in a room with heavy traffic or favored by active children.

Taking these precautions should allow you to enjoy your collection without constantly worrying for its safety.

Storage Tips

The same concerns that apply to displaying your toys also apply to storing them. If you can anticipate problems you can prevent damage.

Most collectors store toys in boxes which they then stack on top of one another. While "free" cardboard boxes are plentiful, avoid them. They may have substances or pests within them that can harm your toys. The ideal storage box will have (a) a reinforced bottom, (b) reinforced sides, and (c) a weight load capacity twice that of the toys you are planning to store in it.

Although the boxes at your local office supply store will not be acid-free, acid-free archival storage boxes are expensive and may not be necessary.

It is critical that you use acid-free or chemically inert material to wrap the surface of your toy before placing it in storage. Two online sources of supply

Old cabinets from department stores, doctor's offices, and jewelry stores are ideal for storing toys. Wall shelves, often mounted floor to ceiling, also are a favored open storage approach. Most toy collectors believe in the premise that open wall space is wasted storage space.

Toy collectors tend to use material available to store their toys. When storing toys in boxes, make certain to use adequate packing to avoid damage from bumping or the stacking of another toy on top.

are www.archivalmethods.com and www.archival supplier.com. Other sources include Hollinger Corporation (PO Box 8360, Fredericksburg, VA 22404), TALAS (920 West 20th Street, 5th Floor, New York, NY 10011), or University Products (17 Main Street, Holyoke, MA 01040).

Once you have securely wrapped the toy you are going to store in acid-free paper, you can use non-acid-free products such as paper, foam peanuts, etc., to secure the toy in place. Use packing supplies such as flexible cardboard ribbon or interlocking cardboard panels to create individual storage sections within a box.

If you are going to stack toys on top of one another, make certain the toys on the bottom can support the weight of the toys placed above. Consider using a sheet of cardboard to divide storage levels and distribute weight within the box.

When storing toys in a box, make a list of what toys are in the box and attach it to the exterior. Make certain the list is visible once the box is placed in storage. It is also useful to note the box's location on the toy's catalog sheet.

While most toy collectors store their excess toys in boxes, those who have the space use shelving. This is known as "open" storage. If you decide to use the open-storage method, make certain you purchase heavy-duty, adjustable industrial shelving. The shelving sold at most office supply stores is not sturdy enough.

Saving money by buying "used" industrial shelving at auction is not saving money at all. You have no way of knowing what was stored on these shelves. Any residue is a threat to your collection.

Line each shelf with acid free paper or mat board to avoid metal-to-metal contact. Consider purchasing sheets or other draping material and hanging it down both sides of the shelves to prevent the accumulation of dust.

It is a good idea to have an exterminator check your storage area for pests once a year. This includes mice, spiders, and similar creatures. If any problems are found, take immediate action.

Finally, do an annual review of the toys you have in storage. Ask the tough question, "Why am I keeping them?" If they are not on display are they really adding to the overall value of your collection? If the answer is no, consider selling them and using the money to buy a toy or toys that you will display.

Toy Restoration

Should a toy be restored to its assembly line appearance or left as it was found, with signs of play and age? The debate continues within the toy community.

In some toy categories such as late nineteenth- and early twentieth-century painted tin toys, pressed-steel vehicles, and pedal cars, the dominant approach is to restore the toy to assembly line quality. In other categories, such as cast-iron toys, collectors assign more value to examples that have "mellowed" with age.

Should the paint on this German hand-painted tin toy boat be restored or not? A toy purist would answer no. Most modern collectors, especially those viewing the toy as an investment, would have the paint restored.

Each collector has to decide whether to restore or not to restore. Although there is no right answer, there are several "correct" approaches if restoration is something you would like to pursue.

If you decide to have a toy restored, use the services of a professional. Avoid the temptation to do it yourself unless you have the necessary skills. The best toy restorers advertise in *Antique Toy World Magazine* (PO Box 34509, Chicago, IL 60634).

There is a difference between restoration and conservation of a toy. Restoration restores the toy to assembly line appearance, including repainting and replacing missing parts. Conservation stabilizes a toy and preserves its present condition. Conservators specialize by material—such as paper, metal, etc. Because of this, it may be necessary to employ more than one conservator to work on a toy. For instance, a painted metal toy may go first to a metal conservator and then to a painting conservator. The best method to locate conservators in your area is to request recommendations from the curators at your local art museum, historic site, or historical society.

Insuring Your Collection

There are several things you will want to accomplish before buying insurance for your toy collection. First, using a video camera or digital camera, record your collection. Do it shelf by shelf or display area by display area. Keep one copy for yourself and place another in a secure location outside your home.

If you can afford it, invest in a quality home security system that provides theft and fire protection. A security system should also reduce your insurance premium.

Security also affects how and where you talk about your toy collection. Be discreet. When talking about your collection, especially in public, never mention value.

Historically, homeowner's policies covered the loss of collections provided their value fell within the loss percentage allowed by the insurer. Today, it is far more likely that your homeowner's policy contains an exclusionary clause limiting the amount of loss the insurer is willing to pay for your toy collection. It is prudent to review your home-

Make a practice of doing room-by-room photographs of your toy collection at least once a year, ideally twice a year. Take detailed shots of your most valuable toys. Store these images outside your home so you have documentation in case of loss from fire or theft.

owner's or renter's policy to clarify whether your toy collection is covered.

If additional insurance is required, you will purchase it as a fine arts rider, which covers fine and decorative arts, or as valuable paper insurance, which covers books and paper ephemera. Do not forget to add in the value of your research library and files when deciding how much coverage you need.

Coverage divides into two main categories—breakage and loss. Most insurance companies provide a quote that includes both. One method to keep insurance costs in check is to only ask for a "loss" quote, provided that you are willing to assume the risk of breakage.

It pays to shop around, as rates differ considerably from company to company. Many large companies prefer not to write fine arts riders, agreeing to do it only reluctantly to retain existing customers.

When dealing with any potential insurer, determine what documentation is required. Some require an appraisal or photographic record, while others do not. If an appraisal is requested, if may only be for objects valued above a specific dollar amount.

Although most homeowner policies will cover toy collections under a marine inland, also known as a fine arts, rider, some large companies do have units that specialize in high-end antiques. And, in this age of specialization, there are now companies who specialize in insuring toy collections. Consider contacting the Antique and Collectibles Association (PO Box 4389, Davidson, NC 28036; www.antiqueand collectible.com), or Collectible Insurance Agency (11310 McCormick Road, Suite 700, Hunt Valley, MD 21031; www.collectinsure.com) Additionally a third group, American Collectors Insurance (PO

LEFT: Toys with which people grew up are often worth more than they think. This 8" Alexander Wendykins dolls with a tagged bridal gown with all accessories, seven different dresses (four tagged), and three hats in an FAO Schwarz exclusive case is worth more than $1,500. Would your household insurance cover it if it was lost or stolen? RIGHT: The chances of breaking the 1969 Colorform Batman Adventure Set are slim to none. Why pay breakage coverage if you do not need it?

Box 8343, Cherry Hill, NJ 08002; www.american collectors.com) provides insurance to a limited number of toy categories—action figures, die-cast, model trains and sets, and teddy bears.

If cost is an issue, consider only insuring the top items in your collection. Do not insure those that are easy and inexpensive to replace. There is little point in spending so much on insurance that you do not have any money left to buy new toys.

In Summary

Once you have disciplined yourself to keep proper records, display and store your toys properly, and protect them against loss, the process becomes second nature. You can then enjoy your collection with the knowledge that you have done your best to ensure its proper care and safety.

Points to Consider

1. Does the policy provide portal to portal coverage—in other words, from the time you buy a toy until the time you dispose of it?

2. Does the policy's protection expand or contract as you add or dispose of toys?

3. Does the policy provide "replacement value," what you would have to spend to buy an identical example on the open market, or is compensation limited to the price you originally paid for the toy?

4. Does the policy take into consideration pair and set value? The loss of a toy in a pair or set is greater than the loss of the individual toy.

5. Does the policy provide for "mysterious disappearance"? Most policies require that theft be proven. Mysterious disappearance is a major problem in collecting.

6. Does the insurance company have the right to repair an object rather than replace it? Collectors prefer replacement.

7. Does the policy have a deductible?

8. What is the discount for having a home security system?

9. What is the cancellation policy?

CHAPTER NINE

PLACES TO FIND TOYS OF DISTINCTION

The vast majority of older toys remain undiscovered—still stored in attics, basements, closets, garages, and sheds. Anyone who claims most toys are in the hands of collectors, historical societies and sites, and museums is mistaken. This is what continues to make the hunt so exciting. New discoveries are made on a daily basis.

Yet collectors, historical societies and sites, and museums have assembled major toy collections that they enjoy sharing with the public. They are great places to research and study toys. Many maintain large reference libraries for the use of their curators and members to research objects in their collections.

Toy Museums

The mid-twentieth century witnessed the growth of specialized museums, museums devoted to one collecting category or theme. There are more than a dozen toy museums in the United States to visit.

Toy museums are divided into two groups, general museums that focus on a specific chronological period and single category museums whose collection is confined to a specific toy

OPPOSITE: Darth Vader action figure storage case.

Lehmann

When collectors talk about German tin toys, Lehmann is the first name that comes to mind. Lehmann, which began in 1881 in Brandenberg, Germany, moved its operations to Nuremberg in 1951.

Lehmann built its reputation on the high-quality production of lithograph tin toys, e.g., boys on bicycles and dancers. Just prior to World War I, it began the production of toy vehicles.

Desiring to introduce motion, Lehmann developed both coil-spring and friction-motion toys, exporting more than 90 percent of the toys that it made. Many of Lehmann's toys were sold in boxes that featured colorful graphic images. As a result, the boxes are as eagerly sought, perhaps even more so than the toys.

collecting category. There are three easy ways to locate these museums. The first is to visit your local library and ask the reference librarian for museum directories. Many provide category indexes. The second is to do an Internet search, narrowed by toy type, time period, or geographic location. Third, do not forget to check museum listings in *Maloney's*, the reference resource discussed in Chapter Four.

Enchanted World Doll Museum (615 North Main, Mitchell, SD 57301). The museum is home to more than 4,000 dolls exhibited in more than 400 different settings. Dolls from the early 1800s exist side by side with contemporary *Star Trek* dolls. Foreign costume dolls comprise approximately half the collection.

Eugene Field House and St. Louis Toy Museum (634 South Broadway, St. Louis, MO 63102). Eugene Field is known as the "children's poet." Several rooms in the house are devoted to the display of toys.

Maine Antique Toy Museum (3506 Route 1, Waldoboro, ME 04572). This museum has a large collection of character, Disneyana, and personality toys, including a large *Lone Ranger* collection. The museum's emphasis is post-1945 toys.

Old Salem Toy Museum (Frank L. Horton Museum Center, South Main Street, Old Salem, Winston-Salem, NC). This museum, part of the Old Salem museums and gardens complex, has a collection of over 1,200 toys spanning from A.D. 225 to 1925. Most of the toys in the collection are from the nineteenth century and Germanic in origin. Thomas A. Gray and Anne Pepper Gray, his mother, assembled the initial collection and are credited as the museum's founders.

Strong National Museum of Play (One Manhattan Square, Rochester, NY 14607). The Strong National Museum of Play, founded on the personal collection of Margaret Woodbury Strong, has more than 500,000 objects in its collection. Its doll and toy collection is one of the largest in the United States. Other collections include advertising memorabilia, home crafts, and souvenirs. The museum reflects Margaret Woodbury Strong's fascination with the common, ordinary objects of daily life. These objects are displayed to help visitors understand the sense of individuality and community Americans have experienced over the past two centuries.

Wenham Museum (132 Main Street, Wenham, Massachusetts 01984). The Claflin-Richards House, circa 1690, contains a large doll, toy soldier, and toy collection plus a model train room with six operating layouts.

Specialized museums

Specialized toy museums, often based in the communities in which the toy was manufactured, are on the rise. Often supported by a national collectors' club, these museums offer a detailed look at a specific toy collecting category.

Visiting specialized toy museums, even if they do not include the toys that you collect, can help you further appreciate the historical context of toys in general. No toy exists in isolation. It is directly and indirectly linked to all the other toys manufactured at the same time as well as its predecessors and the toys it will influence in the future.

The following is only a sampling:

National Farm Toy Museum (110 16th Avenue Ct. SE, Dyersville, IA 52040). The Farm Toy Museum, founded in 1986, is home to over 30,000 farm toys and collectibles. Dave Bell, at the time an employee of Ertl, and Claire Scheibe, founder and past president of Toy Farmer, Ltd., were the founders.

Forbes Galleries (62 Fifth Avenue, New York, NY 10011). Permanent exhibits include Monopoly, toy boats, and toy soldiers. Malcolm Forbes was a leading toy collector. The museum is located in the lobby of *Forbes* magazine's headquarters.

Geppi's Entertainment Museum (301 West Camden Street, Baltimore, MD 21201) The museum, which features over 8,000 toys, is located in the first office of the B&O Railroad. Although heavily focused on toys, it is a pop-culture museum in which you will find everything from Brownie-related collectibles to Beatles memorabilia.

Marx Toy Museum (50 Bloomfield Parkway, Erie, Pennsylvania 16509). This is one of two specialized museums devoted to Marx toys. It opened in 2000, and includes a collection of prototype and production toys. Once a year, the museum holds an employee reunion.

The Official Marx Toy Museum (951 Second Street, Moundsville, WV 26041). Marx had plants in Girard and Erie, Pennsylvania, and Glen Dale, West Virginia. This museum, located near Glen Dale, features displays of more than five decades of Marx produced toys. Museum displays include a Marx Prototype Room and a train display, transportation and service station area, and life-size Western town street front.

National Toy Train Museum (Paradise Lane, Strasburg, Pennsylvania 17579). The National Toy Train Museum has five operating train layouts—O, S, G, HO, and Z gauge. Its extensive collection covers trains from the mid-1800s to the present.

Toy Town Museum (636 Girard Avenue, East Aurora, New York 14052). The Toy Town Museum's permanent collection focuses on toys made by Fisher-Price and other western New York manufacturers between 1930 and 1950. Many other toys also are exhibited. A collection of material relating to early children's television shows originating in Buffalo is of special interest. The museum also hosts an annual Toy Fest in August.

General museums

American toy museums are broad in scope. Many contain additional collections totally unrelated to toys.

Museum of the City of New York (1220 Fifth Avenue, New York, NY 10029). The Museum's toy collection has over 10,000 objects documenting the play patterns of New Yorkers from the Colonial era

Barbie's Origin

Barbie was based on Lilli, a German doll. Lilli was a cartoon character in *Bild Zeitung*, a German daily newspaper. She was created to be an adult sex symbol, as clearly demonstrated by her curvacious figure and sexy clothing.

Ruth Handler bought a Lilli doll for her daughter while shopping in Switzerland. Wishing to create an adult doll for the American doll market, Handler purchased the rights to Lilli. Bud Westmore, a make-up artist at Universal, did a makeover. Lilli's body was resculptured, the joints improved, and her heavy eyelashes, widow's peak eyebrows, and bee-sting lips scrapped.

Handler and her husband Elliott founded Mattel and introduced Barbie, standing 11 ½ inches tall and weighing eleven ounces, to the world at the February 1959 American International Toy Fair.

Barbie's full name is Barbie Millicent Roberts.

Barbie is often referred to by collectors as the "Vinyl Goddess" and the "Billion Dollar Baby." Barbie collector editions often have romantic themes such as Barbie as the Queen of Hearts.

through the twentieth century. The collection includes toys, banks, games, and dolls, among other categories. It is especially well known for its doll house display and the archives from Clare Creations, a New York company that was a leader in the soft toy industry between 1940 and 1985. The current gallery display includes about 300 objects, depending on rotating exhibitions. The toy collection is one of several historic collections within the museum.

Not all museums display their toy collections. The National Museum of American History, part of the Smithsonian, has a toy collection. Its strength is the Kenneth Idle collection, an outstanding group of 1,400 cast-iron and tinplate toys dating from the 1870s through the 1950s donated by Sears, Roebuck and Company. Only rarely has the Idle collection been displayed as a grouping. Rather, the National Museum of American History displays toys throughout its exhibits, using them primarily to illustrate American culture and lifestyle.

National Toy Hall of Fame

A. C. Gilbert's Discovery Village, a children's museum in Salem, Oregon, established the National Toy Hall of Fame in 1998. The museum honors toys that had national significance in the world of imagination and play. By the beginning of the twenty-first century, the National Toy Hall of Fame was outgrowing its quarters.

The National Toy Hall of Fame moved to Strong-National Museum of Play in Rochester, New York, in 2002. The National Toy Hall of Fame is an interpretive gateway into the Strong,

Hasbro presented the press who attended G.I. Joe's 1994 thirtieth birthday party aboard the U.S.S. *Intrepid* berthed in New York with a special edition G.I. Joe.

providing hands-on opportunities and the sharing of toy play memories.

Toys included in the National Toy Hall of Fame are selected using four criteria: (1) icon status, (2) longevity, (3) discovery, and (4) innovation. Icon status recognizes the most-remembered toys. Longevity prevents the addition of a fad toy, such as Beanie Babies. Toys must span multiple generations of children. Because of the Strong's emphasis on play, toys that foster creativity, discovery, and learning through play are admitted. Thus, it comes as no surprise that one of the inductees is the cardboard box. Innovation was introduced to honor those toy designs that profoundly changed play. A toy selected under the innovation criteria does not necessarily have to meet all of the first three criteria.

The general public is invited to nominate toys at the museum, via the Internet, or by mail. An internal advisory committee, consisting of curators, educators, and historians, culls the submitted recommendations. Their list is submitted to a national selection committee whose votes determine the winning candidates.

Current members of the National Toy Hall of Fame include:

Alphabet Blocks	Lego
Barbie	Lionel Trains
Bicycle	Lincoln Logs
Candy Land	Marbles
Cardboard Box	Monopoly
Checkers	Mr. Potato Head
Crayola Crayons	Play-Doh
Duncan Yo-Yo	Radio Flyer Wagon
Easy Bake Oven	Raggedy Ann
Erector Set	Rocking Horse
Etch A Sketch	Roller Skates
Frisbee	Scrabble
G.I. Joe	Silly Putty
Hula Hoop	Slinky
Jack-in-the-Box	Teddy Bear
Jacks	Tinkertoy
Jigsaw Puzzle	Tonka Trucks
Jump Rope	View-Master

Note that many of the inductees are generic toys, such as the bicycle, jacks, and jump rope. It is equally worth noting that some generic toys are brand specific, like the Duncan yo-yo, Lionel trains, and Radio Flyer wagon. Obviously, since the Hall of Fame was started by A. C. Gilbert, it is reasonable to expect the list to include the Erector Set and View-Master.

Ideal's Mr. Machine allowed youngsters to view the toy's mechanical parts. It also could be taken apart and put back together. Mr. Machine was one of Ideal's most popular toys.

Toy memories differ from individual to individual, from generation to generation.

Let's take a brief trip down Toy Memory Lane. Hopefully, as you read the list, many of the toys will trigger a rush of fond memories of the toys of your youth and those of your parents, children, and grand-children.

Nineteenth century

Philadelphia Tin Toy Co. (1850s); Milton Bradley (1860); F. A. O Schwarz (1862); Edward Ives Co. (1860s); Parker Brothers (1883)

European-manufactured toys dominate this period. American manufacturers tested their manufacturing and marketing skill in the areas of cast-iron, paper, and tin toys along with card and board games.

1900–1920

Lionel Trains (1900); Crayola Crayons (1903); Teddy Bear (1903); Schoenhut Circus (1903 to 1909, with many variations over the next twenty years); Model T Ford cast-iron car (1906); American Flyer (1910); Erector Set (1913); Lincoln Logs (1913); Tinkertoys (1913); Raggedy Ann (1915)

American jingoism at the end of the nineteenth century created enthusiasm for American-made products. Many classic American toys, especially toy trains, originated during this period. The period also witnessed the first character-licensed toys, in this instance newspaper cartoon characters. However, European produced, especially German, toys continued to dominate the marketplace.

This Lionel electric diesel engine, No. 318, was first made in 1924. The engine was produced in six different paint and appointment variations.

Nostalgia Lane

1920–1939

Buddy L (1921); Madame Alexander Dolls (1929); Yo-yo (1929); Ideal Shirley Temple Doll (1934); Sorry (1934), Monopoly (1935); Betsy Wetsy doll (1937); View-Master (1938)

World War I pointed out America's dependence on foreign goods. American manufacturers answered the challenge. American cast-iron and pressed-steel toys dominated the American toy market. American doll manufacturers became firmly established. This was the era when movie-licensed toys competed with cartoon-licensed toys. The Depression was a challenge, and several American toy manufacturers failed. However, The Upson Company (TUCO) in Lockport, New York, used its unsold ⅜" wallboard to make puzzles and became one of the premier toy manufacturers of the period.

Competing jigsaw puzzle manufacturers provided local merchants with window broadsides announcing the arrival of a new weekly or monthly puzzle during the late 1932-early 1933 Depression Era jigsaw puzzle craze.

More than half a dozen different American manufacturers produced Raggedy Ann and Raggedy Andy dolls under license from Johnny Gruelle. The Georgene Novelty Company, who held the license from 1938 to 1962, made this 15 inch high, all cloth, Raggedy Ann (above) and Raggedy Andy (left).

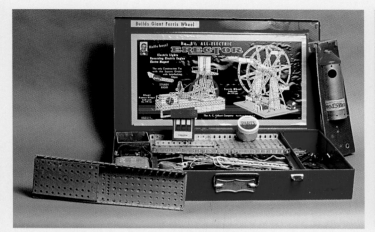

LEFT: This A. C. Gilbert Model 8 ½ All-Electric Erector Set dates to circa 1950. The set allows children to build a working Ferris Wheel and a Giant Power Plant. RIGHT: A very early version of Hasbro's Lite-Brite, #5455, copyrighted 1967. The toy was a huge success when introduced. An early commercial began with the jingle, "Lite-Brite, Lite-Brite turn on the magical shining light." Lite-Brite still is being produced.

1940–1945

American toy manufacturers went to war during this period. Toys were made of cardboard and wood to conserve needed war supplies. Sun Rubber of Barberton, Ohio, a leading manufacturer of rubber toys, made the tubing for pilots' oxygen masks.

E. S. Lowe, a subsidiary of Milton Bradley, issued this version of Yahtzee around the mid-1970s. The instruction booklet has copyrights for 1956, 1961, 1967, 1972, and 1975. The price stick shows an initial sales price of $2.99 reduced to $1.99.

1945–1963

Magic Eight Ball (1947); Tonka Trucks (1947); Slinky (1948), Scrabble (1948); Candy Land (1949); Silly Putty (1950); Mr. Potato Head (1952); Lego Building Sets (1953); Matchbox (1954); Play-Doh (1956); Yahtzee (1956); Frisbee (1957); Hula Hoop (1958); Barbie (1959); Etch A Sketch (1960), Game of Life (1960); Easy-Bake Oven (1963)

This was the beginning of the golden age of television-licensed toys. There was a boxed board game for almost every evening television show. Although magazines facilitated the national promotion of toys, television was the vehicle that reached children. Barbie's success was fueled by a national television advertising campaign. Plastic played an increasing role in all forms of toys. Friction and battery operated toys also became popular.

1963–1980

G.I. Joe (1964); Operation (1965); Twister (1966); Battleship (1967); Lite-Brite (1967); Hot Wheels (1968); Nerf Balls (1970); Atari's Pong (1972); Uno (1972); Dungeons and Dragons (1974); Playmobil (1974); Star Wars Action Figures (1977); Rubik's Cube (1978); Strawberry Shortcake (1979)

Quality is one of the many criteria essential to a classic toy. Alexander, a.k.a. Madame Alexander, has been a prestige brand name for American manufactured dolls for close to a century. This 1953 Alexander 18" Glamour Girl came with a Fashion Academy Award tag.

This era marked the second half of the golden age of television-licensed toys. As the period ends, movie-licensed toys are mounting a serious challenge for shelf space.

The age of the action figure arrives on the scene and challenges vehicles for the heart and soul of young boys. Adventure games such as Dungeons and Dragons enter the marketplace. Pong, Donkey Kong, and Pacman appear, a harbinger of the age of the electronic game toy.

1980 to the Present

Donkey Kong (1981); Cabbage Patch Kids (1983); Trivial Pursuit (1982); Care Bears (1983); My Little Pony (1984); Transformers (1984); Pictionary (1987); Teenage Mutant Ninja Turtles (toy origin 1988, comic origin 1984); Game Boy (1987); Super Soaker (1989); Mighty Morphin Power Rangers (1993);

The 1969s Matchbox Collector's Catalog came in two editions with subtle differences between the two of them. The front cover illustrations showing the cars on the left side of the road must have confused more than one American reader.

Tickle Me Elmo (1996); Beanie Babies (1996); Tamagotchi (1997); Furby (1998); Groovy Girls (1998); Bratz (2004)

This is era of the Big Box Toy store. Lionel's Kiddie City gives way to Toys "R" Us. Today, Wal-Mart is the leading seller of toys.

Toys are no longer launched seasonally. Some manufacturers launch quarterly; others launch year-round. Consolidation becomes the order of the day, ultimately leading to the Big Two—Hasbro and Mattel.

Kenner introduced its first set of *Star Wars* action figures in 1977. The Darth Vader action figure storage case dates from 1980. There also was a See-Threepio (C-3PO) and Laser Rifle action figure storage case.

CHAPTER TEN

YOU ARE A TOY COLLECTOR!

What's Next?

By now, you have probably begun to assemble a toy collection. You have located the childhood toys, which you still have and those stored at your parents' home. Your acquisitions may have included a few toys that belonged to your siblings. If they wanted them, they would have retrieved them long before now, you rationalized. Thinking like this is a clear indication you are well on the way to developing a collector's mentality.

Awareness is one of the keys to collecting. Thinking about toy collecting triggers childhood memories about your favorite toys, but also about toys you wished you had owned but did not. Once you're aware of what you're looking for, the hunt begins. If you have been shopping garage sales, flea markets, and toys shows while reading this book, several of these toys may already be part of your collection. The hunt is simpler when you know what you are seeking.

Advanced collectors often tell new collectors to specialize. Their argument is a simple one: By focusing on one specific toy type, period, or manufacturer, you can maximize your time, funds, and display space. It is good advice, but you should feel free to ignore it for the moment.

OPPOSITE: Toy soldiers lead the parade.

Let your heart dictate what toys you collect initially. If a toy excites you, buy it. If a toy creates a wealth of wonderful childhood memories, buy it. Begin by building an eclectic collection. It takes years, not weeks or months, to understand the toy marketplace. While it's important to gain that understanding, don't let it interfere with the initial euphoria that comes with starting your toy collection.

Specialization will happen eventually whether you plan it or not. A generalist toy collector usually has a dozen or more specialized subcategories within his collection. After a period of general collecting, you may decide there is one subcategory you love more than all others and specialize in it. The collecting skills you learn by collecting on a broader scale become the foundation for the skills you will hone as a specialized collector.

Deciding What to Collect

The old adage of "collect what you like" applies. Your collection reflects your interest and tastes. As such, it is a personal statement. Be open to advice from advanced collectors, but do not allow them to dictate what you collect. There is no right or wrong in collecting. The right decision is the one you make for yourself. The right collection is the one that brings you the most enjoyment.

How do you know what you like? The answer is simple. When a toy group makes you feel happy and puts a grin on your face, take it as a good sign. When you find yourself dreaming about this toy group—and toy collectors do dream about the hunt, their collection, and their wishes—you are hooked. Do not hesitate to follow your dreams.

How many different electric sport action toys did Tudor make? While the Tudor football game is the best know, Tudor also made a baseball, basketball, and race-car version.

Likes and loves can change. When collecting a specific toy type no longer gives you pleasure, look for a new toy group that does. Change often reinvigorates both a collector and his or her collection. Today's collector is far more likely to assemble six or more collections during the time he or she collects than to devote a lifetime to a single collection. The twenty-first century toy market is trendy, and collectors like to keep up with the trends.

Today's toy market is also global. Toys "R" Us has stores in Europe as well as in the United States. While the foreign stores primarily sell the same toys found in the American stores, the packaging is often different. Today a toy collection is not considered complete unless it includes examples from around the world.

Finally, do not forget to collect collectors as well as toys. Toys are fun. So are the individuals associated with them. You will make a host of new friends as your hunt takes you to toys shops and shows throughout the United States and abroad and you surf the Internet. Talk and visit with them.

Learn the History Behind Your Toys

Research turns your toys from inanimate into animate objects. Discover the stories inherent in your toys. When you discover the stories, share them.

Begin the research process by asking some basic questions:

1. Who made the toy?
2. How, where, and when was the toy made?
3. How was it marketed?
4. Who played with the toy and how?
5. How does the toy relate to other toys from the same era?
6. Why did the toy survive?
7. What does the toy say about the person who saved it?

Where do you find the answers to these questions? Begin with the toy reference books and catalogs in your personal library. Then check your local library, historical society, and bookstore for helpful titles you do not own.

Ask relatives and friends what they remember about the toy. If you are lucky, talk to the person from whom you purchased the toy, especially if it is the person who owned it initially. Most importantly, call upon the expertise of members of the toy collecting community.

Consider visiting the town in which the company who manufactured the toy was located. Start by enlisting the aid of the reference librarian at the local public library or historical society. Ask them if they can provide you with the names of individuals living in the community who may have worked for the company. Call them. You will be surprised how willing people are to talk to someone who is interested in them.

Use the Internet. E-mail your questions to potential sources. Run searches. The key to getting desired results is typing in the correct search phrases. Patience is required. Do not become frustrated if your initial search does not produce the results you want. Keep trying.

Who made the Tudor Tru-Action Electric Football Game pictured on page 140? A Google search of "Tudor +Tru-Action" results in several eBay listings for Tudor Tru-Action electronic games. Two of the listing noted the games were made by the Tudor Metal Productions Corporation, Brooklyn, New York. A search of "Tudor Metal Productions Corporation" reveals the company also had a Disney license to produce a Disney character xylophone.

When was this game made? Internet listings indicate the game was introduced into the market in the very late 1940s and was still being made in the mid-1960s. The National Football League licensed later examples.

I know this game was made in the early 1950s because it was one of my childhood games. I received it as a Christmas gift. I played it with my cousins and friends. In the early 1950s, children received only a few toys for Christmas. As a result, many children took care of their toys as a means of extending their playing life.

One toy, dozens of stories! This is true for all toys. All are part of the fun of learning about toys.

Toy soldier collectors like to display their soldiers in real-life dioramas. Some dioramas are replicas of an actual battlefield and can be room-size.

Not all toy information is found so easily. Recent attempts to research a "Build-A-Brik" construction toy created by Peter Gruhn and manufactured by the Allied Toy Company of Valley Stream, New York, yielded no results. I called the reference library and the local historical society. They were not able to help. I did several dozen Internet searches. Again, I had no results. Sometimes, you just have to put a research project aside and come back to it later.

Be an Active Participant

A few toy collectors collect in isolation. They resist interacting with other toy collectors and never share their collection or knowledge. Do not become one of them.

Toy collectors are a vibrant, excited, and fun-loving group. They are an open fraternity, quick to accept new members. All that is needed is a love of toys.

You are familiar with the old adage about the kid in the candy shop. Toy shows are your candy shop. Make a commitment to attend two to four toys shows a year. If you are lucky, there will be a toy show within a few hours driving distance. If not, plan an overnight or long weekend "collecting" vacation.

Think big from the beginning. Put the Allentown Toy Show (Allentown Fairground, Allentown, Pennsylvania) and the Chicago Antiques & Collectible Toy and Doll World Show (Kane County Fairground, St. Charles, Illinois) at the top of your must visit list. Think of these shows as giant shopping malls filled with stores designed to cater to you.

Attend local auctions, especially those whose advertisements list toys for sale. The key is to attend the preview, the day or early morning hours before the auction begins. This is the ideal time to meet other toy collectors. However, a word of advice, do not interrupt collectors when they are inspecting a toy. Wait until they have finished.

Subscribe and attend as many specialized toy

auctions as you can. Even if the toys are valued far beyond your financial means, go anyway. The auctioneer encourages everyone to inspect the toys during the preview. It is a rare opportunity to actually handle high-end toys. Many advanced collectors will be in attendance. Do not be shy. Intermingle. "I am new to toy collecting and would like your advice on how to examine this toy properly" is a perfectly acceptable approach.

Many local historical societies and museums feature toy exhibits as part of their permanent collections and occasionally mount special exhibitions. Visit as many as you can. At some point, take the time to visit the Strong Museum of Play in Rochester, New York, the Mecca for all toy collectors.

Subscribe to all the toy publications that relate to your interests. Set aside time to read them when they arrive. Archive them. As you advance in your collecting, you will find yourself constantly referring back to earlier articles.

The Internet has become an important communication tool. Seek out chat groups, blogs, and other sites that discuss the toys you collect. Be an active participant. In today's environment some "best" friends are individuals known solely via the worldwide web.

Strong National Museum of Play's Library

Toy collectors are blessed with a major research facility: The Strong National Museum of Play's Library. The Library and Archives support the museum's mission—the study of play as it illuminates American culture, through its collection and through the preservation of research materials that document the importance of play with special emphasis on toys and other artifacts related to play. Serving scholars, collectors, and the general public, the library and archives include more then 80,000 books, periodicals, trade catalogs, ephemera, and archival collections covering the period from the early-nineteenth century to the present.

Notable collections include the Stephen and Diane Olin Toy Catalog Collection, consisting of approximately 10,000 catalogs documenting the toy industry from 1960 to the present, and the Brian Sutton-Smith National Archives of Play, the personal library and research papers of one of the most prominent scholars in the field of play research.

The Strong Museum of Play is located in Rochester, New York. The museum is open year-round, but visits to the research library are by appointment only.

Final Thoughts

Think of this book as a roadmap to toy collecting. As you have discovered, there are many highways and byways to travel, and the path you choose and the collection you amass will be a unique reflection of yourself.

Toy collecting is a great hobby. It is an adventure, whether you are hunting, researching, or sharing. Most importantly, it is fun. Collecting toys will bring you a lifetime of pleasure, if for no other reason than it allows the occasional escape of the child inside yourself.

One last reminder. Don't forget to play with your toys. Play captures their heart and soul—and yours as well!

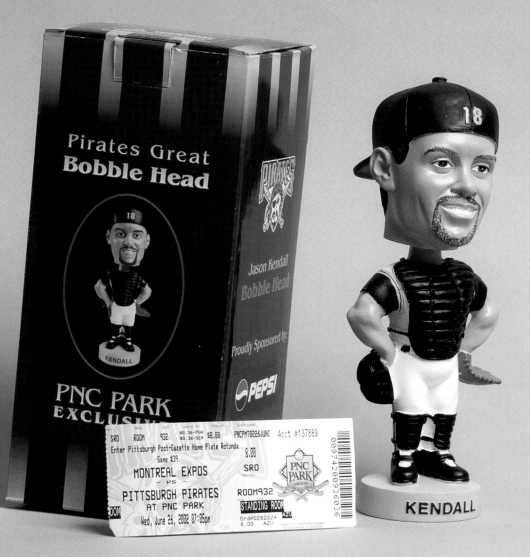

GLOSSARY

Acquisition list a chronological list of your toy purchases annotated with useful details about the purchase of the item.

Action figure general term for posable plastic figures that arrived on the toy scene in the 1960s. Generally they come with a variety of accessories.

BNB term to describe model kits, built but missing its period box.

BWB term to describe model kits, built but still retaining it period box.

Cast-iron toys A material used to make toys, especially in the late 1800s. Cast iron was the material of choice to produce mechanical banks, still banks, cap pistols, and many types of vehicles.

Catalog sheet should contain the toy's acquisition number, name, description, manufacturer and date of manufacture, dimensions, condition, provenance, research information, photograph, purchase information, and date the form was filled out.

Celluloid delicate early plastic material used to make a variety of toys and Christmas ornaments.

Collector Edition toys high-priced, never meant for play, and directed exclusively at the adult market. Often highly speculative.

Complete toys have all their pieces, accessories, period box or blister pack, protective packaging in the box, advertising, instructions, and in extreme cases the shipping box in which the boxed toy was sent.

Composition toys a mixture of pulp, sawdust, and wood chips mixed with glue and pressed into a specific shape.

Condition scale used to rate the quality of a toy or box on a scale from 1 to 10.

Construction toys have many pieces which are used to build imaginative creations. They can be made of a variety of materials such as wood, metal, and plastic.

Copycats stylistic copies of original toys.

Crossover interest refers to toys that are of interest to a number of different types of collectors, such as an action figure that is sought by character collectors, period collectors, and manufacturer collectors.

Die-cast popular toy production method following World War II.

Disneyana a particular collecting category in which only Disney licensed items are collected.

Fantasy items toys that did not exist historically but mimic the design of a period toy.

Jigsaw puzzle a puzzle that assembles into a picture.

Knock-off a generic version of a licensed-product toy often produced during the initial period of an original toy's production.

Letitia Penn A doll brought from Europe to Pennsylvania in 1699, acknowledged by doll collectors as the oldest-surviving doll in the United States. It is named after the daughter of William Penn.

Licensed toy also known as character toys depict characters from movies, TV shows, comic books, and other popular media.

Lithograph printing method used to adhere an image and color to wood or metal toys.

Maloney's reference book that provides information about appraisers, auction sources, buyers, collectors, collectors' clubs, dealers, experts, museums, periodicals, restoration supplies and services, and a wealth of other information for over 3,000 collecting categories.

Mechanical banks highly collectible banks that have moving parts.

Mechanical puzzle a puzzle that require dexterity or mental manipulation to solve.

MIB toy description, mint-in-box.

Miniature collectors different from doll house collectors as historical accuracy and scale are paramount.

National Toy Hall of Fame located in the Strong-National Museum of Play, toys are nominated based on four criteria: (1) icon-status, (2) longevity, (3) discovery, and (4) innovation.

NRFB toy description, never-removed-from-box.

Open storage storing your collection out in the open, such as on shelving.

Pedal car this category includes any pedal toy; including cars but also airplanes, fire engines, tractors, etc.

Period box the original box in which the toy was packed which often lists the available accessories.

Period paint is the original paint job which has not been re-painted or touched up.

Premiums promotional giveaways that either come with a product or are acquired by sending in proof of purchase, sometimes in addition to a small payment.

Pre-school toys refers to toys produced for infants.

Pressed-steel toys A popular material for toy production following World War I.

Provenance is the history of ownership of a toy.

Reissue a toy made from the same die, mold, or printing plate used to create the period toy.

Reproductions exact copies of original toys.

Restoration used to describe a toy that has been returned to the same appearance it had when it was made.

Rinker's Thirty Year Rule "For the first thirty years of anything's life, all its value is speculative."

Scarcity Scale used to rate the scarcity of a toy on a scale from 1 to 5.

Still banks collectible banks that do not have movable parts.

The Big Two refers to the two most dominant toy companies of the twenty-first century, Hasbro and Mattel

Tin plate toys A material used starting in the mid 1800s to make stationary, pull, and clockwork toys. It is made from dipping thin layers of iron or steel in molten tin.

Type collection focuses on depth and breadth by comparing and contrasting similar toys from different manufacturers, locations, etc.

Ultraviolet light a useful tool to spot areas on a toy that have been repainted or repaired.

Variants slight differences in a particular toy produced over an extended manufacturing period, often a change in color or accessories.

Windup toys also known as clockwork toys, began to be produced in the late nineteenth century and must be in working condition to have value.

BIBLIOGRAPHY

Note: Reference for major toy price guides are found in Chapter Four. While some of the books listed in this bibliography do contain price information (often out of date), they have been selected for the research information and history that is part of their content.

General References

Bagdade, Susan and Al. *Collector's Guide to American Toy Trains*. Radnor, PA: Wallace-Homestead Book Company, 1990.

Coleman, Elizabeth A. and Evelyn J. *The Collectors' Encyclopedia of Dolls*. New York: Crown Publishers, 1968.

DeWein, Sibyl, and Joan Ashabraner. *The Collector's Encyclopedia of Barbie Dolls and Collectibles*. Paducah, KY: Collector Books, 1992 value update.

Freeman, Ruth and Larry. *Cavalcade of Toys*. New York: Century House, 1942.

Gardner, Gordon, and Alistair Morris. *The Illustrated Encyclopedia of Metal Toys: An All-Color Guide to the Art of Collecting International Playthings?* London: Salamander Books, 1984.

Herlocher, Dawn. *Antique Trader's Doll Makers & Marks: A Guide to Identification*. Norfolk, VA: Antique Trader Books, 1999.

Hertz, Louis H. *The Handbook of Old American Toys*. Wethersfield, CT: Mark Haber & Co., 1947.

Hertz, Louis H. *The Toy Collector*. New York: Funk & Wagnalls, 1969.

Hirschberg, Morton A. *Steam Toys: A Symphony in Motion*. Atglen, PA: Schiffer Publishing, 1996.

Lavitt, Wendy. *The Knopf Collectors' Guide to American Antiques: Dolls*. New York: Alfred A. Knopf, 1983.

Luke, Tim. *Toys From American Childhood, 1845–1945*. Cumberland, MD: Portfolio Press, 2001.

Matthews, Jack. *Toys Go to War: World War II Military Toys, Games, Puzzles, and Books*. West Missoula, MT: Pictorial Histories, 1994.

McCann, Chris. *Master Pieces: The Art History of Jigsaw Puzzles*. Portland, OR: Collectors Press, 1998.

McClinton, Katharine Morrison. *Antiques of American Childhood*. New York: Clarkson N. Potter, 1970.

Melillo, Marcie. *The Ultimate Barbie Doll Book*. Iola, WI: KP (Krause Publications), 1996.

Miller, G. Wayne. *Toy Wars: The Epic Struggle Between G.I. Joe, Barbie, and the Companies that Make Them*. New York: Random House/Times Books, 1998.

Mullins, Patricia. *The Rocking Horse: A History of Moving Toy Horses*. London: New Cavendish Books, 1992.

O'Brien, Richard. *The Story of American Toys: From Puritans to the Present*. New York: Abbeville Press/Cross River Press, 1990.

Rinker, Harry L. *Collector's Guide to Toys, Games, and Puzzles*. Radnor, PA: Wallace-Homestead Book Company, 1991.

Schwarz, Marvin. *F.A.O. Schwarz Toys Through The Years*. Garden City, NY: Doubleday & Company, 1975.

Sommer, Robin Langley. *"I Had One of Those": Toys of Our Generation*. New York: Crescent Books, 1992.

Whitton, Blair. *Paper Toys of the World*. Cumberland, MD: Hobby House Press, 1986.

Whitton, Blair. *The Knopf Collectors' Guide to American Antiques: Toys*. New York: Alfred A. Knopf, 1984.

Williams, Anne D. *Jigsaw Puzzles: An Illustrated History and Price Guide*. Radnor, PA: Wallace-Homestead Book Company, 1990.

Wulffson, Don. *Toys! Amazing Stories Behind Some Great Inventions*. New York: Henry Holt and Company, 2000.

Specific American Toy References

Beckett, Jeremy. *The Official Price Guide to Star Wars Memorabilia*. New York: House of Collectibles, 2005.

Fox, Bruce R., and John J. Murray. *Fisher-Price: Historical, Rarity, and Value Guide, 1931–Present*. Iola, WI: KP (Krause Publications), 2002.

Freed, Joe and Sharon. *Collector's Guide to American Transportation Toys, 1895–1941*. Raleigh, NC: Freedom Publishing Company, 1995.

Frey, Tom. *Toy Bop: Kid Classics of the 50s & 60s*. Murraysville, PA: Fuzzy Dice Productions, 1994.

Gibson-Downs, Sally, and Christine Gentry. *Antique and Contemporary Toys: Identification & Values*. Paducah, KY: Collector Books, 1995.

Gottschalk, Lillian. *American Toy Cars & Trucks*. New York: Abbeville Press/New Cavendish Books, 1985.

Guild, Kurt, Mike Willyard, and Gary Konow. *Wyandotte Toys Are Good and Safe: A History, Reference & Price Guide to All Metal Products Wyandotte Toys, 1920–1957*. Caledonia, MI: Wyandotte Toys Publishing, 1996.

Hake, Ted. *The Office Price Guide to Disney Collectibles*. New York: Random House Information Group, 2005.

Hanlon, Bill. *Plastic Toys: Dimestore Dreams of the '40s & '50s*. Atglen, PA: Schiffer Publishing, 1993.

Jacobs, Charles M. *Kenton Cast Iron Toys: The Real Thing in Everything But Size*. Atglen, PA: Schiffer Publishing, 1996.

Jaffe, Alan. *J. Chein & Co.: A Collector's Guide To An American Toymaker*. Atlgen, PA: Schiffer Publishing, 1977.

McCollough, Albert W. *The New Book of Buddy "L" Toys, Volume 1 and 2*. Sykesville, MD: Greenberg Publishing Co., 1991.

Moore, Andy and Susan. *The Penny Bank Book: Collecting Still Banks: Through The Penny Door*. Exton, PA: Schiffer Publishing, 1984.

Norman, Bill. *Bank Book: The Encyclopedia of Mechanical Bank Collecting*. Dallas, TX: Taylor Publishing, 1985.

Pinsky, Maxine A. *Greenberg's Guide to Marx Toys, Volume I* (1923–1950) and *Volume II*. Sykesville, MD: Greenberg Publishing Co., Volume I (1998) and Volume II (1990).

Sarasohn-Kahn, Jane. *Contemporary Barbie Dolls: 1980 and Beyond*. Norfolk, VA: Antique Trader Books, 1998.

Wood, Neil S., ed. *Evolution of the Pedal Car*. Five Volume series. Gas City, IN: L-W Book Sales, 1999.

ACKNOWLEDGMENTS

I want to thank Linda K. Rinker, my wife, for her patience and tolerance of a very grumpy old man who mumbled and cursed a lot during the research, writing, revision, and editing process involved in this book. Living with a spouse who is authoring a manuscript and then must fight to preserve its integrity is among the more difficult tests of a marriage's ability to survive. Fortunately, Linda and I are still married.

I strongly suspect more and more writers are going to acknowledge the Internet for its contribution to their efforts. Count me among them. The Internet is a wealth of information—good, bad, and indifferent. I used it heavily—recognizing, of course, that every fact needed to be double and triple checked.

My toy knowledge is an accumulation of interactions with hundreds of auctioneers, collectors, dealers, museum curators, and others as well as exposure to a wealth of toy literature, much of it published after 1980. A general thanks to all for sharing their knowledge with me.

A special thanks to: Dana Morykan, a friend and former Rinker Enterprises, Inc., employee, who proofed the manuscripts and made numerous suggestions to improve it, and David Bausch, the best toy guru in the world.

I also want to acknowledge the support, encouragement, and professional skills contributed by the gang at Band-F—f-stop fitzgerald, Mie Kingsley, and Maria Fernandez.

Thanks to Donna Sanzone and Stephanie Meyers at HarperCollins and Sheila Clark at the Museum of the City of New York.

Finally, special kudos to all the kids—infants, youngsters, juvenile, and adult alike—who understand that toys are meant for play. They have it right.

Have fun,
Harry

PHOTO CREDITS

Photographs on the following pages were taken from the collection at Rinker Enterprises, and are copyright 2007 f-stop fitzgerald inc.: ii, v, vi, 2 top, 3, 5, 6, 8, 11, 13, 14 top, 20, 21, 22, 23, 24, 27 bottom, 32 bottom, 33, 34, 35, 41, 42, 45, 46, 50, 52 bottom, 55, 58, 64 top and bottom, 65, 66, 67, 72, 73, 74, 77, 79, 80, 82 left, 85, 86 left, 92, 99 top, 103, 104, 105 top, 110, 112, 116, 127 right, 128, 134 top, 136, 137 bottom, 140, 144.

Photographs on the following pages were taken at the Dave Rausch Collection, and are copyright 2007 f-stop fitzgerald inc.: 4, 7, 8, 12, 13, 14 bottom, 15, 16, 18, 19 bottom, 26 top, 27 top, 28, 31, 32 top, 39, 48 bottom, 49, 51 bottom, 52 top, 57 bottom, 60, 61 top, 63, 68, 86 right, 88 left, 93 top, 95 bottom, 96, 98 top, 102, 105 bottom, 106, 109 top, 113, 114, 115 top, 117, 118, 120, 123, 124, 126, 134, bottom, 138, 142, 148.

Photographs on the following pages were provided by Rinker Enterprises, and are copyright 2007: 17, 19 top, 26 bottom, 29, 30, 32 middle, 36 bottom left, 38, 40, 43 top, 47, 48 top, 51 top, 54 bottom, 56, 57 top, 61 bottom, 62, 70, 71, 76, 82 right, 83, 88 right, 90, 91, 93 bottom, 95 top, 99 bottom, 101 bottom, 108, 109 bottom left, 111, 115 bottom, 125, 132, 133, 135, 137 top right.

Photographs on the following pages were provided Courtesy of McMasters Harris Auction Company, and are copyright 2007: 2 bottom, 19 top left and right, 36 bottom, 37, 43 bottom, 54 top, 64 center right, 75, 84, 89 right, 95 top, 97, 98 bottom, 100 top left and right, 101 top, 109 bottom right, 121, 122, 127 left, 137 top left.